Brand Comfort Food Classics

A Collection of Favorite
Whole Food, Plant-Based, Oil-Free
Recipes from

Chuck Underwood

Copyright © 2023
Morris Press Cookbooks
All rights reserved. Reproduction in whole or
in part without written permission is prohibited.

Printed in the USA by

800-445-6621 • www.morriscookbooks.com
P.O. Box 2110 • Kearney, NE 68848

Brand New Vegan's Comfort Food Classics
Copyright ©2023 by Chuck Underwood

All Rights Reserved. No part of this publication may be reproduced in any manner without written permission from the author.

Library of Congress Control Number: 2023913497
ISBN: 979-8-9887538-0-3

Food Photography by Chuck Underwood
Cover Design by Chuck Underwood
Cover Editing by Cheryl Overby and Susan Russo
Proofreading by Marian Gonsior, Lisa Hopkins, and Deb Wright
Copyediting by Marian Gonsior and Lisa Hopkins
Recipes by Chuck Underwood & Brand New Vegan, LLC.

Photo Index:

Little Smokies Cocktail Carrots - page 4
Rustic No-Knead Bread - page 9
Brand New Vegan Guacamole - page 11
Vegan Pepper Steak - page 21
Vegan Meatloaf - page 29
Mexican 7 Layer Dip - page 34
Spicy Adobo Potatoes - page 41
Vegan Mapo Tofu - page 51
Perfect Veggie Rice - page 55
Vegan Greek Salad with Tofu Feta - page 61
Vegan Banh Mi Sandwich - page 68
Best Ever Fat-Free Vegan Gravy - page 71
Southern Vegan Green Beans - page 78
Best Damn Vegan Chili - page 81

Dedication

This book is dedicated to all of you striving to make a positive impact on the world, whether that's saving the animals, saving our planet, or saving your own health. Changing your diet and lifestyle isn't easy, but I hope the recipes in this book will give you a great starting point. Many people think that being vegan means eating only salads or boring food, but that's far from the truth. I hope these recipes show you just how delicious and exciting an oil-free, whole food, plant-based diet can be. Here's to your journey of making a difference and enjoying amazing meals along the way.

So to all you "Brand New Vegans," I salute your commitment and applaud your courage. May your journey be filled with joy, fulfillment, and countless delectable discoveries.

Together, let's make a difference in the world, one bite at a time.

Acknowledgements

Thanks to everyone who has supported me over the years. Many of you have been with me from the very beginning, and I just want you to know that without your love, kindness, and support, I wouldn't be where I am today. So from the bottom of my heart, thank you my dear friends.

I also want to thank my BNV Support Group. Your help, suggestions, and feedback in making this book helped immensely. I value our time together and love the little family we have created!

And I especially want to thank my wife Rhonda, who has not only been my partner-in-crime for over 25 years, but is also my biggest supporter and my best friend. Thanks for believing in me honey, I couldn't have done it without you.

About the Author

Chuck Underwood lives in the suburbs of Portland, Oregon with his wife of 26 years, Rhonda.

He became vegan in 2008 when he realized at 46 years old he was NOT the picture of health and was quickly reaching that age where a body's "check engine light" comes on more often than not.

He started his popular blog, *Brand New Vegan*, in 2013 to help others tackle the challenge of changing a lifetime of bad eating habits by recreating the comfort-foods they love - only vegan.

He is a graduate of Dr. T. Colin Campbell's Plant-Based Nutrition Course and has created over 300 comfort-food style recipes that are whole-food, plant-based, and oil-free.

He has tens of thousands of followers who enjoy his 'down-home' cooking style using simple every-day ingredients.

Chuck credits his new diet with saving his life after he suffered a stroke in 2020. Within 24 hours he left the hospital with zero residual effects and within 30 days was completely off all medications.

Chuck frequently speaks at local vegan potlucks and runs a popular Facebook group, support group, and YouTube channel.

A Recipe for the Good Life

A heaping cup of Kindness
Two cups of Love and Caring
One cup of Understanding
One cup of Joyful Sharing

A level cup of Patience
One cup of Thoughtful Insight
One cup of Gracious Listening
One cup of Sweet Forgiveness

Mix Ingredients together
Toss in Smiles and Laughter
Serve to everyone you know
with Love forever after.

Table of Contents

Appetizers & Snacks 1
Breads 7
Dips & Spreads 11
Main Dish - Asian 15
Main Dish - Classics 23
Main Dish - Mexican 31
Main Dish - Potatoes 37
Main Dish - Tofu 45
Multicooker Recipes 53
Salads & Dressings 59
Sandwiches & Wraps 63
Sauces & Gravy 71
Side Dishes 77
Soups & Stews 81
Index 87

Recipe Symbols

Gluten Free    Hot & Spicy    Holiday Favorites

324813-23

Appetizers & Snacks

What to Expect When You Change Your Diet
(*the good & the bad*)

If you are just starting out on a plant-based journey, even if you are just dipping your toes in the water so-to-speak, you will probably begin to experience some common effects soon.

Hopefully, most of the effects will be positive (*weight loss, clothes fitting better, etc.*). But sometimes…. you may not feel so wonderful. But no worries, the negative results usually last just a day or two.

I thought I'd share with you just a sampling of what you might experience, depending on how drastically you are changing your diet.

THE POSITIVES

- Weight loss
- Better fitting clothes
- Clearer skin
- More energy
- Improved sleep
- Improved mood & less anxiety
- Blood pressure drop
- Blood sugar drop
- Cholesterol drop
- Fewer aches & pains
- Your taste buds will change
- Able to reduce certain medications
- And even full disease reversal

THE NEGATIVES

- Diarrhea or constipation
- Cramping
- Bloating
- Lack of energy
- Flu-like symptoms

To counter any of the negative effects, be sure you are drinking plenty of fluids. You can also cut back on the fiber and PLEASE be sure to check with your healthcare provider for any specialized advice to your own unique situation.

APPETIZERS & SNACKS

BBQ CAULIFLOWER WINGS

1 ½ c. cauliflower florets
1 c. unsweetened almond milk
2 tsp. apple cider vinegar
¾ c. flour
¼ c. cornmeal
2 tsp. garlic powder
1 tsp. smoked paprika
½ tsp. thyme
¼ tsp. salt & pepper
⅛ tsp. red pepper flakes
your favorite BBQ sauce
celery and Vegan Ranch
   Dressing, p. 61, for garnish

Preheat oven to 450° F. Line a cookie sheet with parchment paper. Wash cauliflower and break into bite-sized pieces. Mix milk and vinegar together and set aside. Mix all dry ingredients in a large bowl. Add the milk and vinegar mixture to the bowl and stir thoroughly to make a thick batter. Dip each cauliflower piece into the batter and ensure it is evenly coated. Place coated pieces on the cookie sheet and repeat until all pieces are coated. Bake for 15 minutes or until golden brown. Remove from oven and carefully brush on the BBQ sauce. Return to oven and bake for an additional 5 minutes. Serve with celery and vegan ranch dressing on the side.

CRISPY BAKED ONION RINGS

1 lg. sweet yellow onion
1 ½ c. unsweetened almond milk
3 tsp. apple cider vinegar
1 c. flour
2 T. cornstarch
1 c. panko breadcrumbs
1 T. cornmeal
1 T. nutritional yeast
1 tsp. garlic powder
1 tsp. onion powder
½ tsp. salt & pepper
Dash of cayenne pepper (opt.)

Preheat oven to 425° F. Slice onion into ½ inch rings. Mix almond milk and vinegar to make a "buttermilk" and pour over onions in a shallow pan. Cover and soak for at least 1 hour in the refrigerator. Pour off 1 cup of the buttermilk and mix with flour and cornstarch to make a batter. Mix the remaining ingredients in another small pan for the breading. Dip each onion ring in batter and shake off excess. Lay battered onion in breading and with a separate spoon cover it completely with crumbs. Transfer to a cookie sheet lined with parchment paper and repeat. Bake for 20 minutes. Flip rings and bake for an additional 10 minutes. You can also air fry for 10-15 minutes at 350° F. Serve with your favorite dipping sauce.

GRILLED VEGETABLE KABOBS 🥬

Marinade

¼ c. balsamic vinegar
1 T. lemon juice
1 T. Dijon mustard
1 T. maple syrup

1 tsp. minced garlic
½ tsp. onion powder
½ tsp. basil
¼ tsp. salt

Veggies

8 oz. mushrooms
1 red bell pepper
1 green bell pepper
8 baby potatoes

1 onion
1 pkg. or (20 oz.) can pineapple chunks
1 pkg. cherry tomatoes

With the exception of the tomatoes, chop all vegetables and fruit into equal-sized pieces and set aside in a small bowl. Whisk all marinade ingredients together over low heat and simmer for 2-3 minutes or until slightly reduced. Pour marinade over vegetables and fruit and cover. Lightly shake to evenly coat all the veggies and fruit with the marinade and set aside in the fridge. If using wooden skewers, soak in cold water while waiting for the grill to heat up and veggies and fruit to marinate (about 30 minutes). Prepare the grill if using and preheat. Assemble veggies and fruit onto skewers and grill for 8-10 minutes or until potatoes are cooked through. Baste with remaining marinade.

For animals, eating is survival. For humans, eating is a rite of civilization. For Italians, eating is the single great art accessible to us all.
   - Tom Maresca & Diane Darrow, La Tavola Italiana

JALAPEÑO POPPERS 🌶

Vegan Cream Cheese

½ c. raw cashews
7½ oz. tofu
2 T. lemon juice
1 T. apple cider vinegar
1 T. minced pickled jalapeños

1 T. minced chives (or scallions)
¾ tsp. salt
½ tsp. garlic powder
½ tsp. onion powder

Cover cashews with hot water and microwave for 1 minute. Set aside. Drain tofu and cut into cubes. Add to blender. Add remaining ingredients, including drained cashews, to blender. Process until smooth, stopping to scrape down the sides occasionally. Thin with water if necessary.

Poppers

6 lg. jalapeños
1 T. lemon juice
1 c. unsweetened plant milk
1 c. flour
2 T. cornstarch
¼ tsp. salt
1 c. panko breadcrumbs
1 T. cornmeal

1 T. nutritional yeast
1 tsp. garlic powder
1 tsp. onion powder
½ tsp. salt
¼ tsp. black pepper
¼ tsp. cayenne pepper
1 jar red raspberry preserves

Rinse jalapeños and cut off the end with the stem. (Note: Removing the seeds & membranes will cut down on the heat.) Cut each pepper into ¾" "rings" and set aside. Whisk lemon juice and plant milk to make a vegan "buttermilk." In a separate bowl, mix flour, cornstarch, and salt together. Add buttermilk and mix well to make a thick batter. Set aside. Add all remaining ingredients, except preserves, to a large bowl and mix thoroughly to make the breading. Set aside. Stuff each jalapeño ring with the cream cheese, and then dip into the batter ensuring it is evenly coated. Dust coated jalapeño with breading and place in air fryer basket or on a parchment-lined baking sheet. Air fry at 390° F for 15-20 minutes or until browned, or oven fry at 425° F for 30 minutes, flipping halfway through. Serve with red raspberry preserves.

Cookery [has] become an art, a noble science; cooks are gentlemen.
- Robert Burton

LITTLE SMOKIES COCKTAIL CARROTS ❀

1 (16 oz.) bag baby carrots
¼ c. low-sodium soy sauce
¼ c. low-sodium vegetable broth
2 T. maple syrup
1 T. liquid smoke
1 tsp. yellow mustard
1 tsp. minced garlic
1 tsp. pickled jalapeño juice
½ tsp. onion powder
½ c. grape jelly
¼ c. Dijon mustard

Cook carrots by boiling on the stove for 10-15 minutes until just fork tender. Combine the soy sauce, broth, maple syrup, liquid smoke, mustard, garlic, jalapeño liquid, and onion powder to make a marinade. Drain carrots and mix with marinade. Let the carrots marinate in the fridge for a few hours (or overnight), then drain. Add the carrots to a saucepan, mix the jelly and mustard together in a small bowl, and then add to the carrots. Heat gently until bubbly and carrots have heated through. Skewer with toothpicks and serve.

SIMPLE POLENTA BRUSCHETTA ❀

1 (18 oz.) tube prepared polenta
3 tomatoes
2 T. diced onion
4 cloves garlic, minced
1 T. minced fresh basil
2 tsp. balsamic vinegar
½ tsp. salt

Preheat oven to 400° F. Remove the polenta from the tube and cut off the ends. Cut into ½" slices (about 9 of them) and place on a parchment-lined baking sheet. Bake for 15 minutes then flip, and continue baking until golden brown. Meanwhile, dice tomatoes and add to a bowl. Adjust the remaining ingredients to taste and add to the tomatoes. The amounts given were to my liking but you may want more garlic, no onion, less vinegar, no sodium, etc. Feel free to adjust! Remove polenta from oven and top with tomato mixture. Note: Polenta may be air fried too, at 400° F until golden brown.

Why sometimes I've believed as many as six impossible things before breakfast.
- Lewis Carroll, Through the Looking Glass

VEGAN NACHOS SUPREME

Nachos

corn tortillas
squeeze of lime juice
kosher salt
1 c. salsa

1 batch Amazing Vegan Cheese
  Sauce, p. 71
Any or all garnishes

Preheat oven to 350° F. Cut tortillas into equal-sized chips. Arrange chips on a baking sheet and sprinkle with lime juice and kosher salt. Bake for 10 minutes initially, then check every 3-4 minutes until crisp. Add salsa to cheese sauce and blend. Arrange chips on a plate or pan. Cover with some cheese sauce. Add any or all of your favorite toppings. Repeat the cheese and toppings to as many layers as you like. Top with fresh cilantro and vegan sour cream if desired (or more cheese).

Garnishes

Amazing Cauliflower Taco
  Crumbles, p. 23
cherry tomatoes, chopped
green onion slices
red onion slices

black olive slices
jalapeño slices
cilantro, chopped
lime wedges
vegan sour cream

And men sit down to that nourishment which is called supper.
  - William Shakespeare, Love's Labour's Lost

Recipe Favorites

Breads

MY PANTRY

Whole Grains

Eating whole grains is an important part of a whole-food, plant-based diet, along with our fresh veggies, leafy greens, fruit, nuts, seeds, beans, and starches.

And don't think you have to eat strange-sounding grains like quinoa or millet. They ARE nutritious, AND taste good, but you can start simply with the grains you already know.

In MY pantry you will find:

- Corn (*fresh when in season, canned or frozen if not*)
- Wheat (*bulgur*)
- Rice (*white, brown, wild, & black*)
- Oatmeal (*groats, rolled, or steel cut*)
- Brown rice pasta

Products made from whole grains can be healthy too. Just make sure to read the labels and watch for any weird ingredients.

Some of the grain products I keep in my pantry are:

- 100% whole wheat flour
- King Arthur bread flour (*use sparingly as it is refined*)
- Ezekiel bread
- Oil-Free sourdough bread
- Masa flour
- Polenta
- Cornmeal

Other grains & products you might like to try:

- Millet
- Buckwheat
- Quinoa
- Rye
- Barley
- Couscous
- Spelt flour
- Vital wheat gluten

BREADS

HERB CRUSTED PIZZA DOUGH

1 c. warm water
1 T. sugar
2 ¼ tsp. active dry yeast
1 tsp. salt

1 tsp. Italian seasoning
¼ tsp. garlic powder
2 ½ c. bread flour

Mix warm water and sugar together and add yeast. Allow to proof for 10 minutes. Add salt and seasonings and mix well. Add flour and mix until a dough ball forms. Knead with a stand mixer using a dough hook for 5 minutes or by hand for 15 minutes. The dough will be ready when it pulls away from the sides or becomes soft and elastic. Cover with plastic wrap and a towel and allow to rise in a warm oven for 1 hr. Punch down and form into a tight ball. Cover and let rest for 10 minutes. Preheat the oven to 475° F. Stretch dough to fit the pizza pan and place in the oven for 5 minutes. After 5 minutes, remove the pizza dough and add your favorite sauce and toppings. Bake for 10 minutes.

HOMEMADE CORN TORTILLAS

1 c. masa harina
¼ tsp. salt

¾ c. hot water

Whisk masa and salt together in a large bowl. Add water and mix until a smooth, soft dough ball forms. Knead for a few minutes and then cover with a damp towel. Heat a skillet or griddle to medium-high heat. Pinch a walnut-sized piece of dough (1 oz.) and form into a ball. Lay parchment or a cut ziplock bag onto your work surface or tortilla press and place the ball in the center. Cover with more parchment (or ziplock) and gently press into a 5" to 6" round tortilla. Carefully remove paper or plastic and gently lay the tortilla in the skillet. Flip the tortilla after 30-45 seconds. Flip again and cook for 1 minute. Flip again and press with the spatula so the tortilla puffs up, 30 seconds. Flip one last time cooking for 5 to 10 seconds. Wrap tortillas in a towel and allow to steam for 15 minutes before serving.

Herbs do comfort the wearied [brain] with fragrant smells which yield a certain [kind] of nourishment.

- William Coles

HOMEMADE POTATO ROLLS

1 c. unsweetened almond milk
½ c. mashed potatoes
1 T. sugar
2¼ tsp. active dry yeast

1 tsp. salt
¼ tsp. baking soda
¼ tsp. baking powder
2¼ c. bread flour

Stir warm milk, mashed potatoes, and sugar in a mixing bowl until well combined. Add yeast and stir to incorporate. Let rest for 10 minutes for the yeast to bloom. Add salt, baking soda, and baking powder and stir. Add 1 cup of flour and mix until well moistened. If using a stand mixer use the paddle attachment. Add a second cup of flour and mix until the dough ball forms. If using a stand mixer switch to a dough hook attachment. Seal the bowl with plastic wrap and cover with a towel and place somewhere warm to rise. After 1 hour, scrape your dough onto a floured work surface and knead gently. Separate into 16 equal dough balls and place into a 9" x 9" Pyrex dish lined with parchment paper. Cover with plastic wrap and a towel and let rise on top of the stove for an additional 1 hour. Preheat oven to 400° F. Remove the plastic wrap and towel and bake for 17-20 minutes.

OATMEAL APPLESAUCE MUFFINS

1 c. whole wheat flour
½ c. all-purpose flour
1 c. rolled oats
½ c. flaxseed meal
½ c. packed brown sugar
2 tsp. baking powder
1 tsp. baking soda
½ tsp. salt

½ tsp. cinnamon
⅛ tsp. nutmeg
½ c. chopped walnuts (opt.)
1 c. unsweetened almond milk
2 tsp. apple cider vinegar
1 flax "egg"
½ c. unsweetened applesauce
¼ c. molasses

Preheat oven to 350° F. Mix all dry ingredients together in a large bowl, including optional chopped walnuts, if using. Whisk the vinegar and almond milk together in a separate bowl. Add in remaining wet ingredients and stir to combine. Make a well in the center of the dry ingredients and slowly pour in the liquid mixture. Stir until just combined. Pour into prepared muffin tin (or use paper muffin cups) and bake for 15-18 minutes.

Flax Egg

2½ T. water

1 T. flaxseed meal

Add flaxseed meal and water to a dish and stir. Let rest for 5 minutes to thicken.

RUSTIC NO-KNEAD BREAD

3 c. all-purpose flour
1 tsp. salt
½ tsp. instant yeast
1½ c. cold water

In a large bowl, mix all the dry ingredients. Make a well in the center, and slowly add water. Mix until all the flour is incorporated and you have a loose, shaggy dough. Cover and let rise 12 hrs. Turn dough out onto a well-floured surface. Form into a loaf by folding edges in. Place onto a well-floured cloth or parchment paper - seam down - and cover. Preheat oven AND an oven-proof pan and lid to 450° F. CAREFULLY remove pan and lid and place dough inside, seam UP. Replace lid and bake covered for 30 minutes. Remove lid and bake uncovered - an additional 20 to 30 minutes. Let cool and serve.

SIMPLE VEGAN CORNBREAD

1 c. unsweetened almond milk
2 tsp. apple cider vinegar
1 c. cornmeal
1 c. flour (all-purpose or bread)
1 T. baking powder
¾ tsp. salt
¼ c. applesauce
2 T. maple syrup

Preheat oven to 350° F. Whisk the milk and vinegar together and set aside. Sift the dry ingredients together into a large bowl and mix thoroughly. With a large spoon or rubber spatula, slowly stir in the applesauce and maple syrup. Add the vegan "buttermilk" mixture we just made and stir just long enough to make a smooth batter. Pour batter into a parchment-lined pan, seasoned iron skillet, or muffin tins. Bake for 30 minutes or until an inserted toothpick comes out clean.

VEGAN FLUFFY BUTTERMILK BISCUITS

1 c. unsweetened almond milk
2 tsp. apple cider vinegar
2 c. bread flour
1 T. baking powder
½ tsp. baking soda
½ c. Amazing Vegan Cheese
Sauce, p. 71 (chilled)

Preheat oven to 450° F. Whisk almond milk and vinegar together and set aside. Mix all dry ingredients in a large bowl. Add the cold cheese sauce and stir in with a fork until it resembles large crumbs. Slowly pour in the milk mixture and stir with a wooden spoon until just slightly combined. Spoon out onto a floured work surface and gently knead 2-3 times. Roll out dough to 1" thickness and cut circles with a cup, glass, jar, or biscuit cutter. Place biscuits on a parchment-lined cookie sheet so they touch each other. Bake for 15 minutes or until golden brown.

Recipe Favorites

Dips & Spreads

MY PANTRY

Liquids & Condiments

Just like herbs & spices, our liquid "flavor enhancers" and condiments go a long way in making our whole-food plant-based diet foods taste great. Which brands you prefer is totally up to you and may vary by your own specific health needs such as oil-free, no salt, no sugar, etc.

- Apple Cider Vinegar
- Balsamic Vinegar
- Coconut Aminos *
- Dijon Mustard
- Gochujang *
- Ketchup
- Lemon Juice
- Lime Juice
- Liquid Aminos *
- Liquid Smoke
- Maple Syrup
- Marmite *
- Miso *
- Molasses
- Red Wine Vinegar
- Rice Vinegar
- Soy Sauce *
- Sriracha
- Tamari *
- Various Hot Sauces
- Vegan Mayonnaise *
- Vegetable Broth
- Worcestershire *
- Yellow Mustard

* When buying soy sauce, try to find the "low-sodium" version if you can. Coconut Aminos is a good alternative and has the lowest sodium count out of all of them. Tamari is a gluten-free alternative.

* Vegan mayonnaise is extremely high in fat. Use sparingly if you are following a low-fat diet.

* When buying Worcestershire be sure and check the label as it is typically made with anchovies. There are vegan versions available.

* Marmite is a thick, salty paste made from brewer's yeast. It is definitely not for everyone, but I do have it in my pantry.

* Gochujang is a thick paste made from Korean Chile Peppers (gochugaru) and is used in many of my Korean recipes.

* Miso is a fermented soybean paste used in many Asian recipes.

DIPS & SPREADS

BASIC OIL-FREE HUMMUS

2 (15 oz.) cans chickpeas (garbanzo beans)
½ c. aquafaba (liquid from the cans of chickpeas)
4 T. lemon juice
1 T. minced garlic
1 tsp. ground cumin
1 tsp. garlic powder
1 tsp. onion powder
¾ tsp. salt
garnish with sweet or smoked paprika (opt.)

Drain the chickpeas into a bowl and save about ½ cup of the liquid. Rinse the chickpeas thoroughly and add to blender. Add all the remaining ingredients and blend until smooth and creamy, scraping down the sides occasionally. Add the aquafaba a little at a time to get the consistency you like. Garnish with a sprinkle of paprika (sweet or smoked) if desired.

BRAND NEW VEGAN GUACAMOLE

1 clove garlic, minced
⅓ c. minced onion
3 chopped roasted green chiles (or ½ jalapeño)
⅓ c. cherry tomatoes
¼ c. cilantro
3 ripe avocados
½ tsp. salt
1 T. lime juice

Mix the garlic and onion together in a small bowl. Add the chiles, diced tomatoes & cilantro. Mix well then set aside. Cut each avocado in half length-wise and remove the pit. Scoop the flesh of all the avocados into a large bowl. Add salt and lime juice, then mash using a potato masher. Add the onion/tomato mixture and mix well. Taste for seasoning and serve.

CORN BUTTER

16 oz. frozen corn (thawed)
2 T. water
1 T. lemon juice
½ tsp. salt
¼ tsp. garlic powder

Add all the ingredients to a blender and purée until smooth and creamy. Add additional water if needed to get the consistency you like. Use fresh garlic for more of a "garlic butter" taste. Scrape into a pan and simmer on low until slightly thickened.

MEXICAN STREET CORN DIP

Sunflower Aioli

½ (15 oz.) can white beans (liquid reserved)
½ c. raw, shelled, sunflower seeds
2 T. lemon juice
1 tsp. nutritional yeast
2 cloves garlic, minced
¼ tsp. salt
Up to ½ c. of aquafaba (liquid from the canned beans) to thin

Mexican Street Corn Dip

3 (15 oz.) cans fire-roasted corn
¼ c. diced red onion
1 (7 oz.) can roasted green chiles
2 T. salsa
¼ c. cilantro
2 T. lime juice
1 tsp. chili powder
2 T. Sunflower Aioli
¼ c. Vegan Parmesan, p. 75
Lime wedges, additional cilantro, and corn chips for garnish

Prepare aioli by draining the beans and saving the liquid. Add ½ a can of the beans to your blender. Add all remaining aioli ingredients except bean liquid and blend. Scrape down sides as necessary and add just enough bean liquid until the mixture becomes creamy and smooth. Reserve 2 T. of the aioli and place the remainder in a sealed container in the fridge for a tasty sandwich spread. Drain the corn and add to a large frying pan over medium-high heat. Cook corn until the color becomes bright and begins to char (add broth or water to prevent sticking). Add onion, chiles, salsa, cilantro, lime juice, and chili powder and stir until well combined. Stir in the aioli and parmesan and simmer on low heat until heated through. Garnish with lime wedges, additional cilantro, and corn tortilla chips.

The schools of rhetoric and philosophy are empty, but how full the kitchens!

- Seneca

OIL-FREE COWBOY CAVIAR

Dip

1 (15 oz.) can black beans
1 (15 oz.) can chickpeas
5 oz. chopped tomatoes
½ red onion
1 orange bell pepper

1 jalapeño
1 avocado (opt.)
8 oz. corn
¼ c. cilantro

Dressing

⅓ c. aquafaba (liquid from the can of chickpeas)
¼ c. red wine vinegar
2 T. lime juice

3 cloves garlic, minced
¼ tsp. salt
¼ tsp. black pepper

Drain and rinse the black beans and add them to a large mixing bowl. Drain the chickpeas, reserving the liquid, and add them as well. Add the chopped tomatoes. Dice the onion, bell pepper, jalapeño, and avocado (opt.) and add them too - then mix well. Add the corn and the cilantro. Take ⅓ cup of the chickpea liquid and add it and the vinegar to a small bowl. Whisk to combine all remaining dressing ingredients. Pour dressing over the salad and mix well. Cover and refrigerate for 1 hour, then serve.

PIZZA HUMMUS

2 (15 oz.) cans chickpeas
6 T. aquafaba (liquid from the cans of chickpeas)
1 T. minced garlic
4 T. lemon juice
1 ripe tomato

1 T. nutritional yeast
2 tsp. dried oregano
2 tsp. basil
1 tsp. onion powder
1 tsp. garlic powder
¾ tsp. salt

Drain the chickpeas, reserving the liquid and setting the chickpeas aside. Add the aquafaba and remaining ingredients to a blender. Process until well mixed. Add the chickpeas and blend until smooth and creamy. This may take several minutes and you may have to stop and scrape down the sides.

Recipe Favorites

Main Dish Asian

MY PANTRY

Herbs & Spices

Herbs & Spices are the secret to making any meal delicious and are a key part of your vegan pantry. You don't necessarily need to do a complete kitchen makeover when you are first starting out, but as you get used to eating (and shopping) differently you can add new flavors as you go. Most spices lose their flavor after a year, so replace them with new as the need arises.

- Bay Leaves
- Black Pepper
- Cayenne Pepper
- Chili Powder *
- Cinnamon
- Cloves
- Cumin
- Curry Powder
- Dried Basil
- Dried Oregano
- Garlic Powder
- Ground Ginger
- Indian Black Salt *
- Italian Seasoning
- Kosher Salt
- Mexican Oregano *
- Nutmeg
- Nutritional Yeast
- Onion Powder
- Paprika
- Rubbed Sage
- Sesame Seeds
- Thyme
- White Pepper

* American Chili Powder is a blend of paprika, oregano, onion powder, garlic powder, and ground chiles. McCormick is a popular American brand. Be careful of buying chili powder from other countries as it may be 100% chili peppers and will most likely be a LOT spicier.

* Mexican Oregano is a completely different plant from Italian Oregano. You can oftentimes find it in the International Aisle of your grocery store near the dried chile peppers.

* Indian Black Salt (also known as Kala Namak) gives an "egg-like" smell and flavor to many vegan dishes. It's optional but a nice spice to have when you need it.

* Gochugaru are Korean Chile Pepper Flakes and used in some of my recipes. Look for them at Asian markets or Amazon.

MAIN DISH - ASIAN

ASIAN STIR FRY SAUCE

¾ c. low-sodium vegetable broth
3 T. low-sodium soy sauce
1 T. minced garlic
1 T. rice vinegar
1 T. molasses
½ tsp. ginger
1 T. cornstarch
1 T. water

Whisk all the ingredients, except cornstarch and water, over med-low heat until mixture starts to bubble. Mix the cornstarch and water in a separate cup and slowly pour mixture into the sauce. It will start to thicken immediately. Change to low heat, and whisk continuously until you get the thickness you desire.

CREAMY GARLIC MISO NOODLES

16 oz. baby bella mushrooms
1 onion
1 c. low-sodium vegetable broth
4 tsp. minced garlic
½ c. raw cashews
½ c. water
1 tsp. white miso
¼ tsp. garlic powder
¼ tsp. onion powder
¼ tsp. black pepper
12 oz. brown rice spaghetti
1 T. low-sodium soy sauce
green onions, sesame seeds for garnish

Clean and slice mushrooms, and set aside. Dice onion and add to saucepan with veg broth. Cook until the liquid has almost evaporated, then stir in garlic and lightly sauté for 30 seconds. Add the onion & garlic to your blender along with the cashews, water, miso, and spices - BUT DON'T BLEND YET. Set aside for now. Prepare pasta according to package directions. Do not drain yet but remove ½ cup pasta water and add to blender. Now you can blend the sauce until it's smooth and creamy. Add mushrooms to a large sauté pan along with the soy sauce. Cook until their liquid has been released and mostly evaporated. Drain pasta and add it to your mushrooms. Add creamy sauce to the pan and stir to mix well, ensuring everything is coated. Simmer for a minute or two until sauce thickens. Garnish with sliced green onions and/or sesame seeds.

If you own two loaves of bread, sell one and buy a hyacinth.

- Persian Saying

EASY VEGAN PAD THAI

Sauce

- 5 dates
- ½ c. water
- 4 T. low-sodium soy sauce
- 2 T. rice vinegar
- 2 T. lime juice
- 2 T. vegan Worcestershire sauce
- 1 tsp. sriracha hot sauce

Pad Thai

- 8 oz. rice noodles
- 1 (16 oz.) block extra-firm tofu
- ½ white onion
- ½ red bell pepper
- ½ c. baby bok choy
- ½ c. shredded carrot
- 1 tsp. minced garlic
- ½ c. sliced green onions
- ½ c. mung bean sprouts
- crushed peanuts, more green onions, cilantro, and/or sriracha for garnish

Soak noodles in warm water for 30 minutes. Press tofu and cut into 1-inch cubes. Bake or air fry tofu for 15 minutes at 375° F, set aside. Remove pits from dates and add to blender. Blend all sauce ingredients until smooth. Toss baked tofu with sauce and marinate until needed. Dice the onion, pepper, and bok choy. Shred the carrot, mince the garlic, and slice the green onions. Using a little water or veg broth, heat up a pan or wok and add onion, pepper, carrots, and bok choy and stir fry until just softened. Add garlic and stir for 30 seconds. Add sauce and tofu - mix well and cook for an additional 1-2 minutes. Drain noodles and add to the pan - mix well. Add green onions and bean sprouts and stir. Cook 1-2 minutes until veggies and noodles are done. Garnish with crushed peanuts, more green onions, cilantro, and/or sriracha.

EASY VEGAN PEANUT NOODLES

- ¼ c. low-sodium soy sauce
- ¼ c. water
- 8 oz. mushrooms, sliced (opt.)
- 3 T. peanut butter (or PB2)
- 2 T. minced garlic
- 1 T. rice vinegar
- 1 T. maple syrup
- 1 T. hoisin sauce (opt. - adds flavor but more sodium)
- ½ tsp. sriracha (opt.)
- ¼ tsp. ginger
- 8 oz. rice noodles
- 11 oz. frozen vegetables (broccoli & cauliflower)

In a small saucepan, combine all the sauce ingredients (up to rice noodles). If using the optional mushrooms and/or hoisin sauce, add them in this step as well. Heat over low heat until bubbly. Bring about ½ a pasta pot of water to a boil. Add the noodles and cook per package instructions. Microwave frozen veggies per package instructions (or add frozen veggies to the boiling pasta water if you do not want to microwave). Drain completely, stir in sauce, and serve.

HOT AND SOUR SOUP

8 oz. extra-firm tofu
8 oz. shiitake mushrooms
2 c. low-sodium vegetable broth
1 c. water
1 (4 oz) can bamboo shoots (opt.)
3 T. low-sodium soy sauce
1 T. hoisin sauce
3 T. rice vinegar
½ tsp. chile garlic paste
⅛ tsp. white pepper
3 T. cornstarch
3 T. water

Drain tofu and wrap in towels. Cover with something heavy and press for 5-10 minutes. Then cut into ¾" cubes. Rinse and de-stem mushrooms, then slice into strips. Set aside. Bring the veg broth and water to a slow boil in a large soup pot. Add mushrooms, tofu, bamboo shoots (optional), soy sauce, and hoisin. Stir to combine. Let simmer for 3-5 minutes. Stir in vinegar, chili garlic paste, and pepper. Continue simmering for 1-2 minutes. Whisk cornstarch and water together to make a slurry then stir into soup. It should begin to thicken immediately. Stir well and simmer until thickened.

KOREAN BRUSSELS SPROUTS

1 lb. Brussels sprouts
2 T. gochujang Korean chile paste
2 T. rice vinegar
1 T. maple syrup
1 tsp. low-sodium soy sauce
½ tsp. garlic powder

Preheat oven to 400° F. Clean Brussels and cut them in half lengthwise. Parboil or microwave Brussels for 5 minutes. Whisk the remaining ingredients together for the sauce. Drain the Brussels sprouts, coat them with sauce, and arrange them on a parchment-lined baking sheet, cut side down. Roast for 20 minutes. Alternatively, you can also air fry them using the same temp, checking or shaking them after 10 minutes.

It's difficult to think of anything but pleasant thoughts while eating a homegrown tomato.

- Lewis Grizzard

KOREAN MAC N CHEESE 🌶

Cheese Sauce

- ½ c. diced red onion
- 1 T. low-sodium soy sauce
- 2 cloves garlic, minced
- 2 Yukon gold potatoes
- ¼ c. vegan kimchi
- ½ c. water
- 1 T. gochujang paste
- 1 T. onion powder
- 1 T. garlic powder
- 1 tsp. cumin
- ¼ tsp. turmeric
- 1 T. gochugaru flakes
- 3 T. nutritional yeast
- 1 T. pickled jalapeño juice (opt.)
- 1 tsp. rice vinegar
- ½ c. unsweetened almond milk
- 1 tsp. maple syrup

Pasta

- 2 c. brown rice macaroni
- 1 (10 oz.) bag frozen broccoli
- Additional kimchi, sliced green onion tops, and/or sesame seeds for garnish

In a large skillet, add the diced onion and sauté in soy sauce until softened. Add garlic and sauté for 30 seconds. Slice potatoes thinly and add them to the skillet. Add the kimchi and mix well. Add the water & gochujang paste and mix well. Mix the onion powder, garlic powder, cumin, turmeric, and the gochugaru and add to the pan. Stir to mix very well. Increase heat to boil. Reduce heat to low, cover, and simmer for 15 minutes. Carefully add the mixture to a blender along with nutritional yeast, jalapeño juice (opt.), vinegar, milk, and maple syrup. Blend until smooth. Prepare pasta according to package directions. Cook frozen broccoli according to package directions. Drain pasta and return to pot with cooked broccoli and cheese sauce. Mix well. Garnish with additional kimchi, sliced green onion tops, and/or sesame seeds if desired.

Food is not about impressing people. It's about making them feel comfortable.
  - Ina Garten, The Barefoot Contessa Cookbook

MONGOLIAN SOY CURLS

Sauce

3 cloves garlic, minced
1 tsp. ginger, minced
½ c. low-sodium soy sauce
½ c. water

¾ c. date syrup
½ tsp. chile garlic paste (opt.)
⅛ tsp. red pepper flakes (opt.)
1 T. cornstarch

Main Dish

4 oz. soy curls
1 T. soy sauce (opt.)
2 T. cornstarch
1 (10.8 oz.) bag frozen broccoli spears (partly steamed)

sliced green onions and roasted sesame seeds for garnish

Add soy curls to a large bowl and cover with hot water. Add 1 T. of soy sauce if desired to season and set aside. In a saucepan, sauté garlic and ginger in a little water until softened. Add soy sauce, water, and date syrup. Season with chile garlic paste and red pepper flakes if desired. In a small bowl, whisk cornstarch with equal amount of water to create a slurry, then stir into sauce to thicken. Drain soy curls and massage 2 T. of cornstarch into the drained curls, distributing evenly. Add the soy curls to a non-stick skillet. Stir fry until golden brown. Add partly steamed broccoli and sauce and stir to combine. Garnish with sliced green onions and roasted sesame seeds.

Parsley is the crown of cookery. It once crowned man, now it crowns his food.
  - Irma Goodrich Mazza, Herbs for the Kitchen

VEGAN ORANGE CHICK'N

Orange Chick'n

1 sm. head cauliflower
1 c. flour
1 c. unsweetened almond milk
2 tsp. garlic powder
¼ tsp. salt
¼ tsp. black pepper
8 oz. mushrooms, chopped
1 red bell pepper, cut into strips
1 bunch green onions, cut into 1" pieces

Sauce

½ c. low-sodium vegetable broth
⅓ c. rice vinegar
¼ c. brown sugar
¼ c. low-sodium soy sauce
2 T. orange juice
2 T. maple syrup
1 tsp. orange zest
¼ tsp. garlic powder
¼ tsp. ground ginger
2 T. cold water
1 T. cornstarch

Preheat oven to 450° F. Wash and cut a small head of cauliflower into bite-sized chunks. Prepare batter by mixing the flour, milk, garlic powder, salt, and pepper in a large bowl. Dip the cauliflower pieces in the batter until completely covered. Place the dipped cauliflower on a parchment-lined cookie sheet and bake for 20 minutes. Place all sauce ingredients except cornstarch and water in a medium-sized saucepan and bring to a simmer. Whisk cornstarch and water together in a small bowl to make a slurry and add to the sauce to thicken. Add mushrooms to a wok or large pan and stir fry in a little veg broth or water until softened. Add red bell pepper and green onions and continue to stir fry until softened. When the cauliflower pieces are done, stir them into the stir fry and add the sauce. Stir well until everything is completely coated and simmer for a few minutes until heated through.

When one has tasted watermelon he knows what the angels eat.

- Mark Twain

VEGAN PEPPER STEAK ⓥ

8 oz. portobello mushrooms
2 T. + ¼ c. low-sodium tamari
(or soy sauce if not GF)
1 T. + ⅓ c. mirin
1 red bell pepper
1 green bell pepper
1 med. onion

2 cloves garlic
2 tsp. minced ginger
⅓ c. low-sodium vegetable broth
2 T. cornstarch
1 tsp. tahini
¼ tsp. ground black pepper

Clean mushrooms and remove the gills and stems. Slice mushrooms into ¼" strips. Marinate mushrooms in a shallow dish using 2 T. tamari and 1 T. mirin. Stir well to ensure the mushrooms are evenly coated and then set aside. Slice peppers and onion into strips. Mince garlic and add to ginger. In a small bowl, mix all remaining ingredients to make a sauce and whisk until blended. Preheat skillet or wok over high heat. Add garlic, ginger, and a few tablespoons of water and stir fry until fragrant (about 1 minute). Add mushrooms and their marinade and stir fry until the liquid has evaporated. Remove mushrooms from the skillet or wok, and set aside. Add onion and peppers and a tablespoon or two of the sauce. Stir fry veggies until bright and crisp-tender. Return the mushrooms and stir thoroughly. Slowly stir in sauce, mixing well to coat. Simmer until the sauce has thickened.

If you are ever at a loss to support a flagging conversation, introduce the subject of eating.

- Leigh Hunt

Recipe Favorites

Main Dish Classics

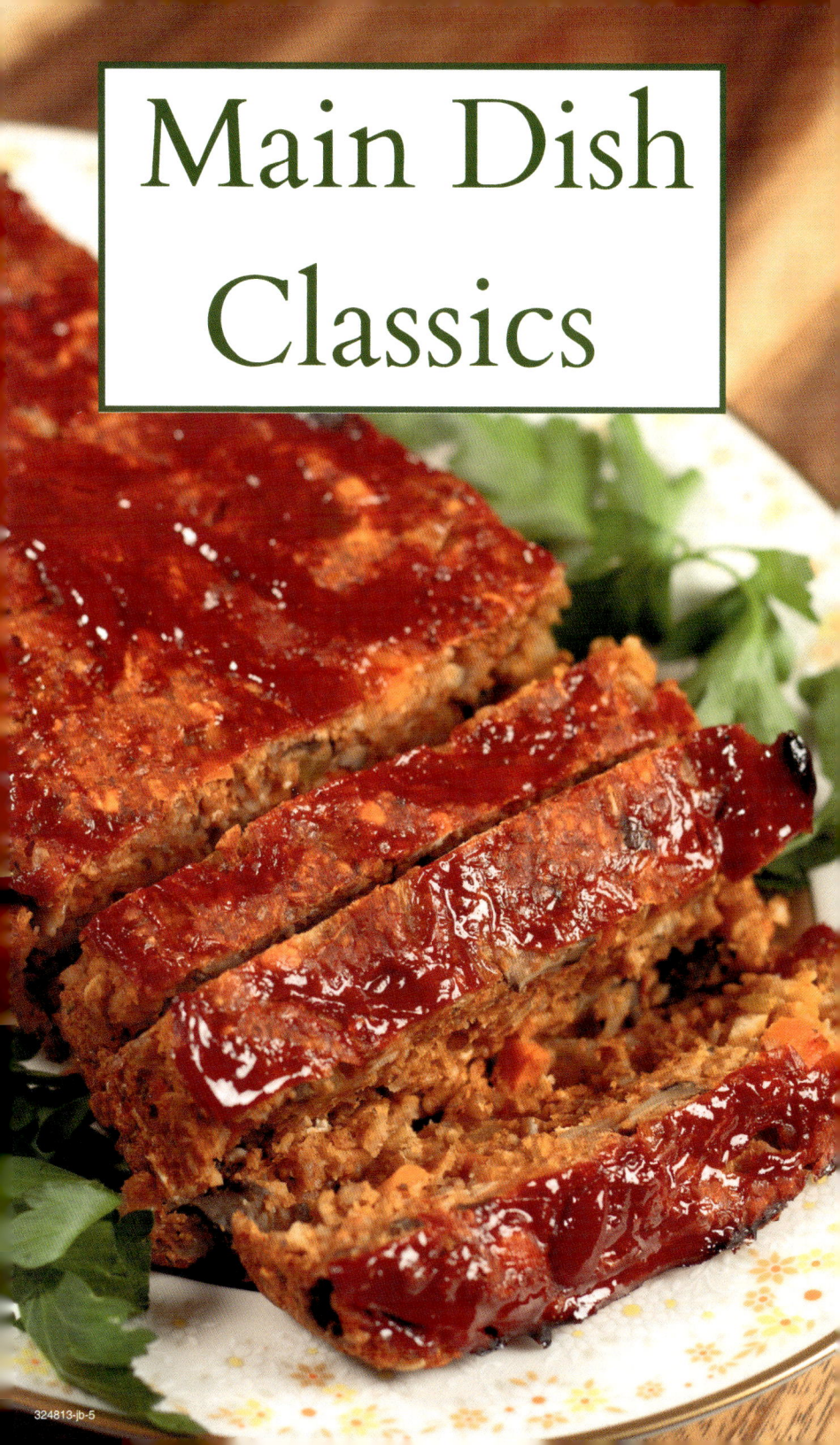

VEGAN SUBSTITUTES

Meat

- **Beans & Lentils** can easily be used in place of meat in many recipes.

- **Portobello Mushrooms** have a savory, umami, and sometimes beefy flavor, especially after being marinated with a little soy sauce.

- **Tofu** (*made from soybeans*) easily absorbs the flavor of any recipe and is a common meat replacement in many of my recipes. Look for organic, non-GMO, extra-firm tofu.

- **Tempeh** (*made from fermented soybeans*) has a crumbly texture and can easily used in place of ground beef in chili and many casseroles.

- **Cauliflower** can either be chopped finely into crumbles or purchased as "Riced Cauliflower". With added herbs and spices, makes an excellent fat-free ground beef alternative for use in tacos, chili, and casseroles.

- **Seitan** is a meat-like substitute made from wheat gluten and flavorings that can be made at home or purchased in select grocery stores.

- **TVP** (textured vegetable protein) is a viable alternative to ground beef but is considered by many plant-based doctors to be a "highly processed" food. I personally do not use it but it is an option you might want to try.

- **Commercial plant-based meat alternatives** are in most grocery stores and come in many forms, from hamburger patties, ground beef crumbles, & chicken nuggets, to sausage patties, bratwurst, and even fish fillets. For similar reasons as TVP, most plant-based doctors do not recommend them due to their excessive processing, sodium amounts, and fat. If you are brand new to eating this way, they are a convenient option but I would recommend you use them sparingly.

MAIN DISH - CLASSICS

AMAZING CAULIFLOWER TACO CRUMBLES

4 oz. mushrooms
½ c. walnuts
1 ½ c. cauliflower (about 1 sm. head)
2 T. low-sodium soy sauce
2 T. chili powder

2 tsp. cumin
1 tsp. smoked paprika
½ tsp. onion powder
½ tsp. garlic powder
¼ tsp. black pepper
¼ tsp. salt

Preheat oven to 350° F. Lightly pulse the mushrooms in a food processor until you have a rice-like consistency. Now pulse (or chop) the walnuts to the same consistency and mix in a large bowl. Remove the core and leaves from your cauliflower and cut it into small pieces. Pulse the cauliflower to the same consistency as the mushrooms and walnuts and add to bowl. Stir in soy sauce and mix. Stir in spices and mix well, making sure everything is mixed thoroughly. Spread the mixture onto a parchment-lined baking sheet and bake for 30 minutes. Stir lightly and continue baking for an additional 10-15 minutes.

CREAMY MUSHROOM STROGANOFF

Tofu Sour Cream Sauce

1 (16 oz.) pkg. silken tofu
¼ c. lemon juice
2 T. red wine vinegar

2 cloves garlic, minced
¼ tsp. salt

Drain the tofu and then add it along with the other ingredients to a blender. Blend until smooth, stopping to scrape down the sides occasionally. If it seems too thick, add a tablespoon or two of water until it reaches a sour cream-like consistency. Note: This makes about 2 cups of sour cream and the recipe only needs one - save the other cup for another use.

Mushroom Stroganoff

½ onion, diced
4 cloves garlic, minced
16 oz. mushrooms, sliced
1 T. low-sodium soy sauce
1 T. vegan Worcestershire

½ c. white wine (or veg broth)
2 tsp. thyme
1 tsp. rosemary
2 c. pasta

Sauté the onion and garlic in a few tablespoons of water or veg broth until softened. Stir in fresh mushrooms and allow to cook down. Add soy sauce, Worcestershire, wine, and seasonings and continue simmering until sauce is reduced. Stir in 1 cup of the sour cream and mix. Set aside. Cook pasta according to package instructions. Drain the pasta and top with the sour cream/mushroom sauce.

CREAMY VEGAN MAC & CHEESE

16 oz. Yukon gold potatoes
1 carrot
½ c. water, reserved from cooking vegetables
6 T. nutritional yeast
2 T. lemon juice
1 tsp. apple cider vinegar

1 tsp. salt
½ tsp. onion powder
½ tsp. garlic powder
½ tsp. yellow mustard
¼ tsp. turmeric
2 c. elbow macaroni
1 (12 oz.) bag frozen broccoli

Wash and scrub both potatoes and carrot, peel if desired. Chop into uniform pieces and boil for 10 minutes or until tender. With a slotted spoon, transfer veggies to a blender. Add ½ cup of the hot potato/carrot water (more if needed to blend smoothly). Pulse to mix. Add in remaining ingredients up to pasta and blend until smooth. Prepare pasta according to package instructions. Add frozen vegetables to last 5 minutes of boiling. Drain pasta, return to pan, and stir in however much cheese sauce you like until creamy and evenly coated.

SAVORY MUSHROOM POT PIE

3 cloves garlic, minced
1 c. diced onion
1 ½ c. low-sodium vegetable broth (divided)
16 oz. baby Bella mushrooms, sliced
¼ c. low-sodium soy sauce
4 ribs celery, diced
4 sm. carrots, diced
1 diced potato, diced

½ tsp. rubbed sage
¼ tsp. thyme
¼ tsp. rosemary
¼ tsp. black pepper
1 tsp. vegan Worcestershire sauce
1 T. tomato paste
¼ c. flour
1 batch Simple Vegan Cornbread batter, p. 9

Preheat oven to 350° F. Sauté garlic and onion in ¼ cup of veg broth. Add mushrooms and soy sauce and simmer until bubbly. Add in vegetables and spices and stir to combine. Add Worcestershire and tomato paste and stir to combine. Allow to simmer, stirring occasionally, until veggies have softened. Sprinkle on the flour and stir. Add remaining veg broth and stir to combine, the stew will thicken immediately. Prepare cornbread batter. Ladle stew to a 15" x 10" baking dish. Spoon cornbread batter over the top to cover. Bake for 30 minutes or until cornbread is golden brown.

SHEPHERDESS PIE

1 batch Amazing Cauliflower
  Taco Crumbles, p. 23
7 russet potatoes
3 ribs celery, diced
1 red bell pepper, diced
1 yellow onion, diced

2 cloves garlic, minced
1 c. frozen corn
1 (4 oz.) can green chiles
2 T. tomato paste
1 c. low-sodium vegetable broth
paprika for garnish

Preheat oven to 350° F. Prepare Taco Crumbles according to the recipe and set aside when done. Peel and cube potatoes and either boil on the stove until fork tender or cook in an Instant Pot with 1 cup of water for 5 minutes. Mash potatoes until creamy, adding veg broth or unsweetened almond milk if needed. Season with salt and pepper to taste and then set aside when done. Meanwhile, sauté celery, red bell pepper, and onion until softened. Add garlic and stir for 30 seconds. Stir in frozen corn and chiles. Mix well and simmer for 2-3 minutes. Add tomato paste and veg broth and simmer until slightly thickened. Stir in the taco crumbles and mix well. Spoon the mixture into a 9" x 13" glass casserole dish and top with mashed potatoes. Smooth evenly, garnish with paprika if desired, and bake for 30 minutes. Cut into squares and serve.

TACO PIE

Enchilada Sauce

1 (8 oz.) can tomato sauce
1½ T. chili powder
¼ tsp. cumin
¼ tsp. onion powder

¼ tsp. garlic powder
⅛ tsp. black pepper
1½ c. water
2 T. cornstarch

Taco Pie

1 batch Amazing Cauliflower
  Taco Crumbles, p. 23
1 onion
1 green bell pepper

1 red bell pepper
4 cloves garlic, minced
1 batch Simple Vegan
  Cornbread batter, p. 9

Prepare the Taco Crumbles according to its own recipe. (p.23). Preheat oven to 350° F. Mix all of the enchilada sauce ingredients except the corn starch in a small saucepan and heat until bubbly. Slowly stir in cold water. Whisk cornstarch with a little water in a small bowl to make a slurry and then add to saucepan to thicken sauce. Set aside 1 c. of the sauce. Set aside. Sauté onion & peppers until softened, then stir in minced garlic just until fragrant - about 30 sec. Stir in taco crumbles and add the cup of enchilada sauce and stir to combine. Cook until bubbly and slightly thickened, and then remove from heat. Spoon the mixture into a 9" x13" glass baking dish and spread evenly. Prepare the cornbread batter then spread it evenly over the casserole. Bake for 30 minutes or until golden brown.

VEGAN CHICK'N & DUMPLINGS

Chick'n & Broth

2 T. low-sodium soy sauce	8 oz. mushrooms, sliced
½ tsp. poultry seasoning	½ tsp. thyme
1 c. water	½ tsp. rosemary
4 oz. soy curls	½ tsp. salt
1 med. onion, diced	¼ tsp. black pepper
2 cloves garlic, minced	4 c. low-sodium vegetable broth
3 med. carrots, diced	1 bay leaf
3 ribs celery, diced	1 tsp. apple cider vinegar
3 baby gold potatoes, diced	

Dumplings

1½ c. flour	2 T. parsley
½ c. cornmeal	½ tsp. salt
1 T. baking powder	1½ c. unsweetened almond milk

Whisk the soy sauce and poultry seasoning into the cup of water and pour over soy curls to rehydrate for about 10 minutes. Sauté onion and garlic in a couple of tablespoons of broth until softened. Add diced carrots, celery, and potatoes and cook until softened. Add sliced mushrooms and spices and cook until softened. Add drained soy curls, broth, bay leaf, and vinegar, and bring to a boil. Meanwhile, mix flour, cornmeal, baking powder, parsley, and salt. Stir in almond milk until a batter is formed. Slowly drop in spoonfuls of batter for as many dumplings as you want. Cover pot and simmer for 15 minutes or until dumplings are done. Any remaining batter can be placed in muffins tins and baked as biscuits - 350° F - 15 minutes.

A day out-of-doors, someone I loved to talk with, a good book and some simple food and music – that would be rest.
- Eleanor Roosevelt

VEGAN CHICK'N POT PIE

Vegan Chick'n

1 c. low-sodium vegetable broth
2 T. low-sodium soy sauce
½ tsp. poultry seasoning
2 c. soy curls

Pot Pie Filling

2 carrots
2 ribs celery
½ white onion
½ c. low-sodium vegetable broth
2 Yukon gold potatoes
½ tsp. minced garlic
¼ tsp. thyme
¼ tsp. salt
¼ tsp. black pepper
¼ tsp. turmeric
1 pinch rubbed sage
¼ c. all-purpose flour
2½ c. low-sodium vegetable broth
⅓ c. frozen peas
1 batch Vegan Fluffy Buttermilk Biscuits dough, p. 9 (opt.)

Whisk together 1 cup of veg broth, the soy sauce, and the poultry seasoning in a medium-sized bowl. Stir in soy curls and set aside, stirring occasionally. Chop carrots, celery, and onion and add to a large soup pan. Sauté in ½ cup broth until softened. Dice potatoes and add to the pan along with garlic, and stir to combine. Cook for another minute. Add thyme, salt, pepper, turmeric, and sage and stir well. Add the soy curls and stir to combine. Sprinkle flour into the stew and stir. Continue cooking for 1 minute. Slowly stir in 2½ cups of veg broth and increase heat to a low boil. Mixture should begin to thicken. Remove from heat and stir in peas. If eating as a stew, let rest for 5-10 minutes and serve. If using biscuit topping, preheat oven to 375° F and prepare biscuit dough using the recipe. Arrange biscuit rounds on top of the filling and bake for 25-30 minutes or until the biscuits are browned.

VEGAN HAMBURGER HELPER

1 batch Amazing Vegan Cheese Sauce (3 c.). p. 71
1 batch Amazing Cauliflower Taco Crumbles (2½ c.), p. 23
1 (12 oz.) pkg. pasta
1 (10 oz.) pkg. frozen broccoli/cauliflower mix
1 (14 oz.) can diced tomatoes
salt & pepper to taste
green onions for garnish

Prepare cheese sauce according to recipe directions and set aside. Prepare taco meat according to recipe directions and set aside. Prepare pasta according to package instructions, adding frozen veggies to pasta water to cook with pasta once it's boiling. Drain pasta and veggies and return to pan. Stir in tomatoes, taco meat, and finally, the cheese sauce. Adjust any seasoning and heat until warm and bubbly. If desired, top with thinly sliced green onions.

VEGAN LASAGNA WITH TOFU SPINACH RICOTTA

10 lasagna noodles
1 (10 oz.) box frozen spinach
¼ c. raw cashews
1 batch Oil-Free Marinara Sauce, p. 73
16 oz. extra-firm tofu
2 cloves garlic, minced
2 T. lemon juice
1 tsp. apple cider vinegar
¼ c. nutritional yeast
1 tsp. Italian seasoning
½ tsp. salt
¼ tsp. black pepper

Preheat oven to 325° F. Cook lasagna noodles according to package instructions. Thaw spinach and soak cashews in water. Prepare marinara sauce. Drain and press the tofu to remove as much moisture as possible. Add cashews, tofu, and garlic to a food processor and pulse until it resembles ricotta cheese. Add remaining ingredients to processor and pulse to mix well. Add rinsed and drained spinach and give mixture a few more pulses until combined. Assemble the lasagna by adding about 1 cup of sauce to the bottom of a rectangular lasagna pan. Add the first layer of noodles, sauce, and ricotta. Add a second layer of noodles, sauce, and ricotta. Add a third layer of noodles and cover with the remaining sauce. Bake for 30 minutes.

No man in the world has more courage than the man who can stop after eating one peanut.

- Channing Pollock

VEGAN MEATLOAF ★

Veggies

- 2 c. diced onion
- 2 ribs celery
- 2 med. carrots
- 1 sm. sweet potato
- 8 oz. portobello mushrooms
- 1 T. low-sodium soy sauce
- 2 tsp. minced garlic

Grains

- ½ c. bulgur
- ¼ c. water
- ½ c. rolled oats
- ½ c. panko bread crumbs
- ¼ c. flaxseed meal
- 1 tsp. onion powder
- 1 tsp. smoked paprika
- ¾ tsp. thyme
- ¾ tsp. rubbed sage
- ½ tsp. poultry seasoning
- ½ tsp. salt
- ¼ tsp. black pepper
- ¼ tsp. white pepper
- 2 T. tomato paste
- 1 (15 oz.) can chickpeas
- ketchup or your favorite sauce for garnish

Preheat oven to 350° F. Add bulgur and ¼ cup of water to a shallow dish. Set aside. Prep all veggies by dicing them into evenly-sized ¼ cubes. Slice mushrooms and sauté in soy sauce just until liquid is released. Add the diced veggies and cook until the veggies have softened and the liquid has evaporated. Add garlic, stir, and remove from heat. Allow to cool. In a large bowl, add all the Grain ingredients including the bulgur we set aside earlier and reserving the tomato paste and drained chickpeas until last. Mix thoroughly using a fork or potato masher. Add all the cooked veggies and continue mixing and mashing to the desired consistency. Line a 1.5 qt. Pyrex loaf pan with parchment paper. Add meatloaf mixture to loaf pan compressing as you go. Smooth the top and brush on ketchup or your favorite sauce. Bake for 1 hour. Remove from oven and allow to cool for 30 minutes. Remove from loaf pan, and slice. Garnish with ketchup or your favorite sauce.

Sharing food with another human being is an intimate act that should not be indulged in lightly.

- M.F.K. Fisher

Recipe Favorites

Main Dish Mexican

Scoville Heat Unit

This is simply a chart to give you an idea how hot or spicy one Chile pepper is compared to another.

The peppers or sauces that are in BOLD letters are the ones I use the most in my recipes. The higher the number, the hotter the pepper.

Another good rule of thumb: The SMALLER the pepper, the spicier it is.

Scoville Heat Unit Chart

Pepper	Min	Max	Avg SHU
Bell	0	0	0
Pepperoncini	100	500	**300**
Frank's Hot Sauce			**450**
Pimento	100	1,000	550
Paprika	100	1,000	550
Gochujang			750
Salsa Lizano			1,000
Poblano	1,000	1,500	**1,250**
Ancho	1,000	1,500	**1,250**
Anaheim	500	2,500	1,500
Pasilla	1,000	2,500	1,750
Huy Fong Sriracha			**2,200**
Tapatio Sauce			**3,000**
Cholula Hot Sauce			**3,600**
Tabasco Sauce	2,500	5,000	**3,750**
Guajillo	2,500	5,000	3,750
Huy Fong Chile Garlic	2,500	5,000	**3,750**
Hatch Chile	1,000	8,000	4,500
Jalapeno	2,500	8,000	5,250
Chipotle	2,500	8,000	5,250
Gochugaru Flakes	1,500	10,000	5,750
Fresno Chiles	2,500	10,000	6,250
Serrano	10,000	23,000	16,500
Chile de Arbol	15,000	30,000	22,500
Cayenne	30,000	50,000	40,000
Thai	50,000	100,000	75,000
Habanero	100,000	350,000	225,000
Ghost	855,000	1,041,427	948,214
Carolina Reaper	1,400,000	2,200,000	1,800,000
Pepper Spray	2,000,000	5,300,000	3,650,000
Pure Capcaicin	15,000,000	16,000,000	15,500,000

MAIN DISH - MEXICAN

BLACK BEAN TOSTADAS WITH GREEN CHILE SOUR CREAM

Green Chile Sour Cream

1 c. cashews
¼ c. hot water + hot water to soak cashews
2 tsp. apple cider vinegar
2 tsp. lemon juice
½ tsp. salt
½ tsp. red wine vinegar
4 whole Hatch green chiles

Soak cashews in enough hot water to cover completely for at least 30 minutes. Place remaining ingredients--including drained cashews--in blender and blend on high until smooth, scraping down the sides occasionally.

Black Bean Tostadas

1 (15 oz.) can black beans (no salt added)
½ (15 oz.) can vegetarian refried beans
¼ tsp. onion powder
¼ tsp. garlic powder
¼ tsp. ground cumin
¼ tsp. chipotle chili powder
1 tsp. masa harina corn flour (opt.)
corn tortillas
roasted red bell peppers for garnish
diced tomatoes for garnish
shredded lettuce for garnish

Turn on your broiler to 450° F. Place all bean ingredients in a pot and stir to combine. Add the masa to thicken if desired. Toast corn tortillas on a cookie sheet for 2-3 minutes at a time before flipping. Repeat until crispy. Place the bean mixture on the tostada shell and spread evenly. Top with garnishes and chilled sour cream.

Man does not live by words alone, despite the fact that sometimes he has to eat them.

- Adlai E. Stevenson

CHEESY HASH BROWN ENCHILADAS

1 batch Amazing Vegan Cheese Sauce, p. 71
1 batch Easy NM Red Chile Sauce, p. 32
1 (20 oz.) pkg. shredded hash brown potatoes
½ onion, diced
½ red bell pepper, diced
½ poblano pepper, diced
1 tsp. minced garlic
4 corn tortillas

Prepare cheese sauce and red chile sauce and set aside 1 cup of each. Preheat oven to 350° F. In a large bowl, mix potatoes, onion, peppers, and garlic. In a 9" x 13" glass baking dish, spread ½ cup of red chile sauce across the bottom. Add 2 of the corn tortillas, side by side. Add ½ of the potato mixture and flatten with a spatula. Spread ½ cup of cheese sauce. Add 2 more tortillas. Spread ½ cup red chile sauce. Spread remaining potatoes. Spread the remaining cheese sauce. Bake uncovered for 45 minutes or until potatoes are cooked through. Garnish with your favorite toppings.

EASY NEW MEXICAN RED CHILE SAUCE (ENCHILADA SAUCE)

20 New Mexican red chile pods
¼ med. white onion, roughly chopped
2 c. water
1 (8 oz.) can tomato sauce
2-3 cloves garlic
½ tsp. garlic powder
½ tsp. onion powder
½ tsp. Mexican oregano
½ tsp. cumin
¼ tsp. salt

Preheat oven to 250° F. Arrange 20 chile pods on a cookie sheet and roast for 20 minutes. Flip chiles halfway through the roasting process. After chiles have cooled to the touch, remove stems and seeds. Add chiles and onion to a large pasta pot and cover with water. Bring to a boil, then reduce heat, cover, and simmer for 10 minutes. Strain the chiles, reserving 2 cups of the chile water for blending- as long as it is not bitter. If it is too bitter - discard the water and use fresh water when blending. Carefully remove chiles and onion from the pot and add to the blender. Add remaining ingredients and blend until smooth.

If more of us valued food and cheer and song above hoarded gold, it would be a merrier world.

- J. R. R. Tolkien

GALLO PINTO (VEGAN RICE & BEANS)

1 c. diced onion
1 c. diced red bell pepper
½ c. diced tomatoes
1 tsp. minced garlic
1 (15 oz.) can black beans
2 T. salsa Lizano
¼ c. cilantro
2 c. cooked rice (cold)
Additional cilantro, chopped onions, or sauce for garnish

Add 1 cup of diced onion to a skillet with 1-2 T. water/veg broth to prevent sticking. Sauté on medium heat for 1 minute, stirring frequently. Add pepper and continue sautéing for 1 minute, stirring frequently. Stir in tomatoes and sauté 30 seconds. Add garlic, stir, and cook for 2-3 minutes. Drain beans and add them to the pan. Stir in 2 T. of the salsa and the cilantro. Finally, add the cooked rice and stir well to combine, breaking up any clumps. Cook until heated through. Garnish with additional cilantro, chopped onions, or sauce.

HATCH GREEN CHILE SAUCE

2 c. Hatch green chiles, chopped
½ c. onion
4 cloves garlic, minced
¼ tsp. cumin
½ tsp. Mexican oregano
½ tsp. salt
½ tsp. black pepper
2 c. low-sodium vegetable broth
1 T. cornstarch or arrowroot (for thickening)

Preparing the Hatch chiles: If they are already roasted, carefully removing the outer skin, membranes, and seeds, before chopping. If they are not roasted, lightly roast them over your BBQ grill or under your oven's broiler until the skins have blistered and blackened in spots, rotate frequently. Then sauté the onion in a few tablespoons of water or broth until softened. Stir in minced garlic and simmer for 1 minute. Add spices and simmer until bubbly, then stir in your peeled and chopped chiles. Add broth and simmer. Blend to desired consistency. Whisk cornstarch or arrowroot with 2 T. cold water to make a slurry, then stir into sauce to thicken.

You don't have to cook fancy or complicated masterpieces – just good food from fresh ingredients.

- Julia Child

MEXICAN 7 LAYER DIP

1-2 c. Amazing Vegan Cheese Sauce, p. 71
1 (15 oz.) can fat-free refried beans
1 (15 oz.) can pinto beans
2 lg. avocados
3 green onions, chopped
2 cloves garlic, minced
2-4 T. lime juice (divided)
cilantro, chopped (divided)
salt to taste
3 diced tomatoes
¼ white onion, chopped
1 jalapeño (or 1 (4 oz.) can green chiles for a milder spice)
lettuce, tomatoes, black olives, vegan sour cream for garnish

Prepare cheese sauce and set aside. Warm the beans in a small saucepan until bubbly. Prepare guacamole by mashing avocados, green onions, garlic, 1-2 T. lime juice, and cilantro together. Prepare Pico de Gallo by mixing tomatoes, onion, jalapeño, remaining lime juice, and remaining cilantro together. Spread bean mixture in a glass casserole dish. Layer on the cheese, followed by the guacamole, and then the Pico de Gallo. Top with shredded lettuce, chopped tomatoes, black olives, and vegan sour cream if desired. Refrigerate or enjoy immediately.

MEXICAN PASTA SALAD

Chipotle Dressing

½ c. unsalted hulled sunflower seeds
1 c. water (divided)
1-2 chipotle peppers with 1-2 tsp. adobo sauce
2 cloves garlic
2 T. apple cider vinegar
1½ tsp. maple syrup
1 tsp. smoked paprika
½ tsp. salt

Soak the sunflower seeds in ½ cup of water for 30 minutes. To a blender, add the sunflower seeds and the soaking water, the other ½ cup water, and all the remaining dressing ingredients and blend until smooth and creamy. Note: You will have to scrape down the sides a few times.

Salad

6 oz. gluten-free fusilli pasta
1 (15 oz.) can black beans
1 c. corn
¾ c. cherry tomatoes
3 green onions
1 (4 oz.) can roasted green chiles
1 small handful cilantro or baby spinach

Prepare pasta according to package directions (my package was 12 minutes). Drain and rinse pasta and place in large bowl. Rinse and drain beans and add to pasta. Add the corn, tomatoes, and chopped onions and mix well. Add all the remaining salad ingredients and mix well.

POSOLE

4 oz. soy curls (½ bag)
8 c. water (divided)
½ white onion
5 green onions
1 Yukon gold potato
4 cloves garlic, minced
1 (2.5 oz.) bag red chile pods
 (guajillo or New Mexican)
2 tsp. cumin

½ tsp. black pepper
½ tsp. salt
1 (30 oz.) can white hominy
 (maiz blanco)
3 tsp. Mexican oregano
½ tsp. garlic powder
2 bay leaves
4 c. low-sodium vegetable broth

Bring soy curls and 4 cups of water to a boil. Simmer for 4 minutes. Strain, press, and dry the soy curls to remove as much moisture as you can, then add to a hot skillet. Gently fry the soy curls for about 5 minutes until they begin to brown then set aside. Dice the onions, green onions, and potatoes, and mince the garlic. Clean chiles by removing stems, heads, membranes, and seeds. Add chiles to 4 cups boiling water and simmer for 4-5 minutes or until softened. Reserving 1 ½ cups of the chile water, transfer just the chiles to a blender. To the blender, add the 1 ½ cups of chile water-as long as it is not too bitter (use fresh water in that case), garlic, cumin, pepper, and salt, and blend until smooth. Add chile sauce to a large pot or Dutch oven and cook for 5 minutes, stirring often. Add drained and rinsed hominy, onions, green onions, potato, oregano, garlic powder, bay leaves, and veg broth. Mix well. Simmer for 30 minutes. Add the cooked soy curls and simmer for an additional 15-20 minutes.

SOPA DE FIDEO

1 (7 oz.) pkg. fideo noodles
 (vermicelli)
1 med. onion
3 c. low-sodium vegetable broth
2 cloves garlic, minced

1 (28 oz.) can San Marzano
 whole tomatoes
1 tsp. Mexican oregano
½ tsp. cumin
½ tsp. chili powder

Toast pasta in a dry baking pan at 350° F for 10 minutes, or until slightly browned. Dice onion and add to a large soup pan. Sauté in 1-2 T. veg broth until softened. Add oregano, cumin, chili powder, and minced garlic and stir until fragrant - about 30 seconds. Add the tomatoes with their juice and stir to mix. Simmer for a minute or so and then blend the entire contents of the pan either in a regular blender or with an immersion blender. Add broth and stir to mix, then add noodles. Simmer for 20 minutes, stirring occasionally, until the noodles have softened.

Recipe Favorites

Main Dish Potatoes

MY PANTRY

Frozen Foods

Frozen fruit & vegetables are literally the NEXT best thing to fresh, followed by canned.

However, be careful when buying frozen veggie mixes that include any kind of sauce, as many of those sauces usually include unwanted ingredients. You truly just want the veggies or fruit, nothing else.

If the sauce comes separate in a packet – fine as we can throw that away.

Here is a just a sample of some of the items I keep in my freezer:

- Active yeast (*for making bread & pizza dough*)
- Applesauce
- Aquafaba (*the juice from canned chickpeas*)
- Bags of spinach & kale
- Bell pepper slices
- Blueberries
- Broccoli & Cauliflower
- Chipotle peppers & adobo in ice cube trays
- Commercial fruit mixes
- Commercial packages of mixed veggies (*without sauce*)
- Ezekiel bread
- Freshly roasted green chiles
- Ginger root
- Homemade veggie burgers
- Jalapeno peppers
- Leftover batch cooked rice
- Leftover servings of soups, stews, sauces, etc.
- Nuts, seeds, soy curls, & flour
- Peas & corn
- Shredded potatoes or hash browns
- Tofu (*freezing tofu changes the texture*)
- Tomato paste in ice cube trays for a single serving
- Veggie scraps (*for making broth*)
- Ripe bananas (*for nice cream*)

MAIN DISH - POTATOES

BREAKFAST POTATOES

1 med. sweet potato
2 Yukon gold potatoes
1 tsp. salt
¼ onion
½ red bell pepper
2 cloves garlic, minced
8 oz. crimini mushrooms
1 T. low-sodium soy sauce
½ tsp. garlic powder
½ tsp. onion powder
½ tsp. kala namak Indian black salt (can sub. salt)
¼ tsp. black pepper
2 c. leafy greens (spinach, kale, etc.
Easy NM Red Chile Sauce, p. 32, and cilantro for garnish

Dice the potatoes into ½" cubes and add to a large pot. Add enough water to cover and 1 teaspoon of salt. Bring to a boil and let simmer for 3-5 minutes, then remove from heat. Add the diced onion and bell pepper to a large skillet and sauté in 2 T. of veg stock or water just until softened. Add the minced garlic and stir just until fragrant - about 30 seconds. Add the sliced mushrooms and cook just until they begin to lose their water, then drain the potatoes and add them along with the seasoning. Stir to combine and heat on med-high heat until the skillet begins to look dry or the potatoes start to brown. Remove from heat and add 2 cups of your favorite greens, then cover until the greens wilt. Stir and serve with your garnish of choice. I added a little bit of my red chile sauce and cilantro, and it was divine!

COTTAGE FRIES

1 T. salt
4 qt. water
4 med. Yukon gold potatoes
1 T. apple cider vinegar
Seasoning:
2 T. panko breadcrumbs
1 T. nutritional yeast
1 tsp. onion powder
1 tsp. garlic powder
1 tsp. paprika
¾ tsp. salt
¼ tsp. black pepper

Preheat oven to 425° F. Add 1 T. salt to 4 qt. water and bring to a full rolling boil. Meanwhile clean and cut potatoes into ¼" thick rounds. Place potatoes in a bowl of cold water until ready. Whisk all the seasoning ingredients together in a small bowl and set aside. Drain your potatoes and carefully add them to the boiling water. Add the apple cider vinegar and set your timer to 10 min. When finished, carefully drain your potatoes and rinse with cold water. Place potatoes in a ziplock with 2-3 T. of the seasoning mix and shake to coat. Place the coated rounds on your baking sheet or air fryer basket. Air fryer/convection oven: 8-10 minutes at 425° F or until crispy. Reg oven: 15-20 minutes or until crispy. Serve with your favorite fry sauce.

CRISPY OVEN-BAKED FAT-FREE FRENCH FRIES

7 med. potatoes
1 T. flour
1 tsp. garlic powder
1 tsp. onion powder

1 tsp. paprika
1 tsp. chili powder
salt & pepper to taste

Preheat oven to 425° F and line cookie sheet with parchment paper. Clean and slice potatoes into fairly thick french fries ¾" to 1" thick. Add to pot of cold water (enough to cover) and bring to boil. Boil for 5 minutes. After boiling, drain potatoes and place back into the pot. Add all seasonings, cover, and shake to distribute. Spread evenly on a cookie sheet and bake for 20-25 minutes.

EASY DEVILED POTATOES

12 sm. baby gold potatoes
1 (15 oz.) can chickpeas
4 T. aquafaba (liquid from can of chickpeas)
2 cloves garlic, minced
3 T. lemon juice

1 T. Dijon mustard
¼ tsp. onion powder
¼ tsp. cumin
¼ tsp. turmeric
salt and pepper to taste
paprika for garnish

Preheat oven to 400° F. Scrub potatoes and slice in half. Lay evenly, cut side up, on a cookie sheet, and bake for 40 minutes. Drain the chickpeas, reserving the liquid, and rinse. Add chickpeas to a blender along with garlic, lemon juice, mustard, and spices. Pulse until thoroughly mixed. Add 1 T. aquafaba at a time - until desired consistency. Add more lemon juice and/or mustard to taste. Salt and pepper to taste. Once potatoes are finished baking, allow them to cool, and then carefully scoop out the center. Save the potato centers, or eat them. Using a pastry bag (or ziplock bag), fill hollowed-out potatoes with hummus. Garnish with paprika and serve.

FAT-FREE POTATO CHIPS

2 russet potatoes
pinch garlic powder

pinch onion powder
pinch kosher salt

Wash and scrub your potatoes before slicing if leaving the peel on. Using a mandoline or whatever slicing device you may have, thinly slice the potatoes into chips. Lay chips in a single layer on a sheet of parchment paper. Sprinkle seasonings evenly over the chips. Microwave for 5-7 minutes, watching closely. Stop when they begin to turn a golden brown.

FUNERAL POTATOES

Topping

½ c. old-fashioned rolled oats
2 T. nutritional yeast

½ tsp. garlic powder

Casserole

1 (28 oz.) bag frozen hash browns
1 ½ c. Amazing Vegan Cheese Sauce, p. 71
1 med. onion, diced
2 (7 oz.) cans roasted diced green chiles

½ tsp. cumin
½ tsp. garlic powder
½ tsp. salt
½ tsp. black pepper
green onions for garnish

Preheat oven to 375° F. Begin thawing frozen potatoes. Make the cheese sauce according to the recipe instructions. Sauté onion in 1-2 T. of veg broth or water. In a large bowl, mix potatoes, chiles, cooked onion, cheese sauce, cumin, garlic, salt, and pepper. Pour out into a 9" x 13" casserole dish. Cover with foil and bake for 30 minutes. Mix topping ingredients and grind them if you want more of a powder. After 30 minutes, remove the foil from the casserole, sprinkle topping evenly over top, and continue baking for an additional 6-8 minutes. For a crispier topping, turn on the broiler for the last 5 minutes - watching carefully. Once done, garnish the potatoes with sliced green onion tops.

Everyone is kneaded out of the same dough but not baked in the same oven.

- Yiddish Proverb

HASH BROWN PIZZA CUPS

Potato Cups

1 (20 oz.) pkg. shredded hash brown potatoes
1 tsp. Italian seasoning
¼ tsp. salt

¼ tsp. black pepper
2 T. flaxseed meal
3 T. hot water

Pizza Filling

1 c. mushrooms
½ c. onion
¼ c. red bell pepper
¼ c. Ultimate Fat-Free Pizza Sauce, p, 73

garnish: Amazing Vegan Cheese Sauce, p. 71, panko breadcrumbs, sliced green onions, or your choice

Preheat oven to 475° F. Prepare Pizza Sauce according to the recipe, and set aside. In a large bowl, combine the potatoes and seasonings. Whisk flaxseed meal and hot water and let rest 2-3 minutes, then mix this in as well. Press ⅓ cup potato mixture into a muffin tin to form each cup. Bake the potato cups for 15 minutes. Meanwhile, finely dice the mushrooms, onion, and bell pepper. Add veggies to a small bowl and stir in ¼ cup of the pizza sauce. When the potatoes are done, remove the pan from the oven, and carefully spoon 1-2 tsp. of the veggie and sauce mixture into each cup. Continue baking for an additional 10 minutes. Once again remove the pan from the oven and this time, set the oven to broil. Garnish with cheese sauce, panko, green onions, and whatever topping you want. Broil for 1-2 minutes.

POTATO ENCHILADAS

2 lg. Yukon gold potatoes
½ white onion
¼ c. low-sodium vegetable broth
2 cloves garlic, minced
4 oz. mushrooms, sliced
½ tsp. chili powder

¼ tsp. black pepper
small handful fresh spinach
1 ½ c. Easy NM Red Chile Sauce, p. 32
8 corn tortillas

Preheat oven to 350° F. Prepare Easy NM Red Chile Sauce, p. 32, and set aside. Cube potatoes and boil for 5 minutes until softened. Drain potatoes and set aside. Finely dice the onion and sauté in veg broth until softened. Add minced garlic and stir. Add mushrooms and cook until they have reduced in size. Stir in spices and finely chopped spinach - it will wilt quickly. Add the potatoes back in. Stir in ½ cup enchilada sauce. Heat tortillas to soften. Spread another ½ cup of sauce into a 9" x 13" baking dish. Spoon 1-2 T. of potato mixture into each tortilla, roll, then lay seam-side down in the baking dish. Cover with remaining enchilada sauce. Cover the dish with foil and bake for 30 minutes. Garnish with your favorite toppings and serve.

SMASHED POTATOES WITH GARLIC AIOLI

1 (24 oz.) bag baby gold
   potatoes
Salt & pepper to taste

Vegan Garlic Aioli Sauce, p.74
Garnish: chopped green onion

Boil potatoes in a large pot of water until fork tender - 25-30 minutes OR you can also use your Instant Pot: add 1 cup of water and potatoes, set to secure lid, set to SEALING, cook on MANUAL for 5-7 minutes, then quick release. Drain potatoes and let sit for 5 minutes. Preheat oven to 350° F. Smash potatoes flat and lay on a parchment-lined baking sheet. Bake in the oven for 30-40 minutes or until edges get crispy OR Air fry at 325° for 15-20 minutes. Serve with garlic aioli and garnish with chopped green onions.

SPICY ADOBO POTATOES

½ c. Vegan Garlic Aioli Sauce,
   p. 74
½ c. Easy NM Red Chile sauce,
   p. 32

3 c. Yukon gold potatoes
Garnish: favorite hot sauce and
   fresh cilantro

Preheat oven to 400° F. Prepare aioli according to recipe instructions and keep refrigerated until needed. Prepare red chile sauce. Cube potatoes into ½" squares and place on a parchment-lined baking sheet. Roast potatoes for 10 minutes. Using a spoon, mix and toss the potatoes with the red chile sauce until evenly coated. Continue roasting for an additional 10-15 minutes. Place into a serving dish and top with aioli and your favorite hot sauce. Garnish with fresh cilantro leaves.

I doubt whether the world holds for anyone a more soul-stirring surprise than the first adventure with ice cream.
- Heywood Broun

VEGAN POTATO SOUP WITH GREEN CHILES

- 1 yellow onion
- 2 med. carrots
- 2 ribs celery
- 3 cloves garlic, minced
- 1-2 (8 oz.) cans chopped green chiles
- 4 russet potatoes
- 2 c. low-sodium vegetable broth
- 2 c. water
- 1 tsp. chili powder
- ½ tsp. cumin
- ½ tsp. salt
- ¼ tsp. black pepper

Finely dice the onion, carrots, and celery and add to a large soup pot. Sauté the veggies in a few tablespoons of veg broth or water until softened. Stir in 3-4 cloves of minced garlic and simmer 30 seconds. Add 1-2 cans of green chiles and simmer 2-3 minutes. I'd start with one and try it first, then maybe add the 2nd. Add diced potatoes, veg broth, water, and seasoning and stir well. Bring the soup up to a good, medium simmer and cover for at least 15-20 minutes or until the potatoes are cooked all the way through. Carefully - remove 2 or 3 ladles of soup and purée in a high-speed blender before adding back into the soup. Purée more if you like a smoother soup, but I like chunks of potatoes left in mine. Adjust seasoning if needed and serve.

As a child my family's menu consisted of two choices: take it or leave it.

- Buddy Hackett

VEGAN SWEET POTATO CASSEROLE ★

Casserole

2 ½ lbs. yams (orange sweet potatoes)	½ tsp. salt
¼ c. unsweetened almond milk	½ tsp. cinnamon
1 T. lemon juice (or apple cider vinegar)	½ tsp. vanilla
	⅛ tsp. nutmeg

Peel and cube sweet potatoes and add them to a large pot of cold water. Add a generous pinch of salt, heat to boiling, cook 10 minutes (or until fork tender), drain, and return to pan. In a small measuring cup or bowl, whisk almond milk and lemon juice together. Then slowly mix in salt, cinnamon, vanilla, and nutmeg. Pour into potatoes and mash until creamy. Spoon into a casserole dish and smooth out the top.

Topping

1 c. roasted, salted pistachios	½ tsp. cinnamon
1 c. rolled oats	1 T. maple syrup
¼ tsp. salt	1 banana

Preheat oven to 350° F. Roughly chop 1 cup of roasted, salted pistachios and place them in a small bowl. Also rough chop, pulse, or lightly grind the oats and mix them into the pistachios. Stir in the salt and cinnamon, mix, and then stir in the maple syrup. Mix well. Finally, slice a banana and using a fork, mash it into the crumb mixture, being sure to incorporate it very well. Mix until there are no dry crumbs left. Carefully crumble the topping onto your casserole, being sure to cover as much of it as possible, and lightly pressing down topping with a fork. Bake for 25-30 minutes.

When baking, follow directions. When cooking, go by your own taste.

- Laiko Bahrs

VEGAN SWEET POTATO CHILI

- 1½ lbs. yams (orange sweet potatoes)
- 1 T. aquafaba (liquid from a can of beans)
- ½ tsp. salt
- ½ tsp. smoked paprika
- 1 white onion, diced
- 1 red bell pepper, diced
- 3 cloves garlic, minced
- 1 T. minced pickled jalapeños (opt.)
- ¾ tsp. cumin
- 1 T. chili powder
- ½ tsp. oregano
- 2 (15 oz.) cans fire-roasted tomatoes
- 1 c. water
- 1 T. cornmeal (or masa harina)
- 1 tsp. molasses
- 1 tsp. unsweetened cocoa
- 2 (15 oz.) cans black beans

Preheat oven to 400° F. Cube sweet potatoes and add to a bowl. Add aquafaba, salt, and paprika and toss to coat. Roast for 20 minutes - set aside to cool. In a large Dutch oven, sauté onion and pepper until softened. Add jalapeño if desired and garlic - stir to mix well. Stir in cumin, chili powder, and oregano - simmer for 5 minutes. Add tomatoes, water, cornmeal, molasses, and cocoa. Bring heat up to medium and simmer for 30 minutes - stirring occasionally. Drain and rinse black beans and add to chili. Add roasted sweet potatoes and taste for seasoning. Add salt if needed and serve with your favorite garnish.

Age does not diminish the extreme disappointment of having a scoop of ice cream fall from the cone.
- Jim Fiebig

Main Dish Tofu

MY PANTRY

Canned (and Jarred) Goods

Canned goods are the next best thing to buying fresh or frozen and you can save a lot of money when items go on sale.

Let's face it – we know how bad grocery store tomatoes can be, especially in the winter, so canned tomatoes are the next best thing to picking them right off your own vine.

I always have a supply of canned goods including beans, tomatoes, and green chiles ready to go in my pantry for quick & easy meals.

- Artichokes
- BBQ sauce
- Canned beans (any variety)
- Canned fruit in their own juices
- Canned mushrooms
- Canned pineapple
- Chipotle peppers in adobo sauce
- Corn
- Diced, crushed, whole, fire-roasted tomatoes
- Diced green chiles
- Green beans
- Green chile sauce
- Olives
- Peas
- Pickled cucumbers
- Pickled jalapenos
- Pumpkin
- Salad dressing (Maple Grove Farms)
- Sun-dried tomatoes (in water)
- Tomato sauce & paste
- Vegetable broth
- Water chestnuts

MAIN DISH - TOFU

BBQ TOFU BURNT ENDS

Basic Rub

¼ c. sweet paprika
2 T. kosher salt
2 T. chili powder
2 T. brown sugar
1 T. black pepper
2 tsp. garlic powder
2 tsp. onion powder
½ tsp. cayenne pepper

Mix all rub ingredients together until uniform and store in an airtight container until needed. I used a 1-pint mason jar with a lid.

Burnt Ends

1 (16 oz.) pkg. extra-firm tofu
1 T. apple juice
2 T. Basic Rub
Your favorite BBQ Sauce

Freeze tofu prior to making the recipe (not absolutely necessary but highly recommended), then thaw before continuing. Drain the tofu and slice it into 2 even blocks about 1" thick. Press tofu between paper towels for at least 30 minutes. While the tofu is being pressed, preheat the oven to 300° F. Once the tofu is finished being pressed, slice each block into 12 equal cubes and place them in a ziplock bag with the apple juice. Shake gently. Add 2 T. of the rub to the bag and again, shake gently to ensure all surfaces of tofu are covered. Bake on parchment-lined baking sheet for 15 minutes. The tofu is now ready for the BBQ. Place over indirect heat and gently brush on your favorite sauce. Turn frequently and continue basting until a nice bark has formed on the outside of each cube.

It's so beautifully arranged on the plate – you know someone's fingers have been all over it.

- Julia Child

CHICK'N FRIED TOFU

Cream Gravy

¼ c. flour
1 T. nutritional yeast
1 tsp. rubbed sage
½ tsp. salt

½ tsp. black pepper
1 pinch thyme
3 c. unsweetened almond milk

Whisk all dry gravy ingredients together and then pour into a large skillet. Toast dry ingredients for 1-2 minutes over med-low heat, then slowly stir in 3 cups of almond milk. Whisk to remove any lumps and stir often as mixture begins to thicken. Once the mixture has thickened to a thick, gravy-like consistency, remove from heat and set aside. (It will thicken even more - thin with more almond milk if necessary.)

Batter & Breading

14 oz. extra-firm tofu
Breading:
1 c. panko breadcrumbs
1 T. paprika
2 tsp. garlic salt
1 tsp. dried mustard
1 tsp. celery seed
½ tsp. white pepper
½ tsp. salt
½ tsp. thyme

½ tsp. basil
Batter:
½ c. chickpea flour
½ tsp. onion powder
¼ tsp. salt
¼ tsp. black pepper
2 tsp. lemon juice or apple cider vinegar
1 c. unsweetened almond milk

Drain tofu and slice into 3 equally-thick steaks (about ½" thick). Wrap the tofu pieces in paper towels and place something heavy on top to press out as much moisture as possible. Press and drain for at least 20 minutes, changing paper towels as needed. Whisk all the dry breading ingredients together in a bowl, then spread evenly in a flat, shallow pan for dredging. Set aside. Whisk all the dry batter ingredients together in a small bowl. Also, whisk either lemon juice or vinegar into almond milk to make a "buttermilk." Pour into the dry ingredients and mix until smooth. Pour batter into a flat, shallow pan and set aside. Preheat oven to 400° F and place a wire cooling rack on top of a baking sheet. With one hand place a tofu steak into the batter. Brush the batter to make sure it's evenly coated. With the same wet hand, place the battered tofu into the breading. Using your other (dry) hand, spoon or scoop the breading evenly over the tofu until evenly coated. Place tofu steaks on the wire cooling rack on the pan and bake until brown and crispy, about 30 minutes. Spoon on gravy and serve.

EASIEST VEGAN STIR FRY EVER

Sauce

¼ c. low-sodium vegetable broth
¼ c. low-sodium soy sauce
2 T. rice vinegar
2 T. maple syrup

1 T. minced garlic
1 T. minced ginger
3 tsp. sriracha
1 T. cornstarch

Stir Fry

14 oz. extra-firm tofu
16 oz. baby bella mushrooms
12 oz. pkg. frozen stir fry vegetables

1 c. sauce

Make the sauce by adding all the sauce ingredients to a mason jar, attaching the lid, and shaking thoroughly. Next, press the tofu to remove as much moisture as possible, and cut it into cubes. Using a 1 qt. mason jar, marinate the tofu cubes in the sauce, - at least 1 hour. Drain tofu and reserve sauce. Bake or air fry the tofu - at 375°F - about 20 minutes total - flipping midway. Clean mushrooms and cut them in half. Add mushrooms to wok with a splash of veg broth or water - turn the heat to high. Once the broth begins to boil, add frozen veggies and stir fry just a few minutes - until crisp-tender. Add baked tofu cubes and the remaining sauce. Stir until the sauce has thickened. Serve over your favorite rice.

Life expectancy would grow by leaps and bounds if green vegetables smelled as good as bacon.

- Doug Larson

GARLIC PANKO TOFU

Sauce

4 T. maple syrup
3 T. low-sodium soy sauce
2 T. rice vinegar
4 tsp. mirin

2 tsp. gochugaru Korean chile flakes
1 T. cornstarch

Tofu & Veggies

your choice of prepared pasta, rice, or potatoes
1 (12 oz.) block extra-firm tofu
1 (10 oz.) pkg. frozen vegetables
¼ red onion
2 green onions
2 tsp. low-sodium soy sauce

1 tsp. garlic powder
½ tsp. onion powder
2 T. panko breadcrumbs
¼ tsp. salt
6 cloves garlic, minced
1 (6 oz.) can sliced mushrooms, rinsed and drained

Preheat oven to 400° F. Prepare rice, pasta, or potatoes. Press tofu for 30 minutes. Whisk together the sauce ingredients and set aside. Microwave frozen veggies and chop, if necessary. Chop onions and set aside. Cut tofu into cubes and place in a ziplock bag along with 2 teaspoons soy sauce. Gently toss to coat. Whisk tofu spices with the panko and add to bag. Again - gently toss to coat. Air fry (or bake) tofu for 10 minutes. Sauté onion, green onions, and garlic in a little water or veg broth until softened and aromatic. Add mushrooms and cooked frozen veggies and stir. Add sauce. Add air-fried or baked tofu and stir to ensure everything is evenly coated. Serve over rice, pasta, or potatoes.

MY GRANDSON'S FAVORITE TOFU

10 oz. block extra-firm tofu
¼ c. low-sodium soy sauce
¼ c. low-sodium vegetable broth
1 T. minced garlic
2 T. rice vinegar

2 T. maple syrup
2 T. cornstarch (divided)
1 tsp. smoked paprika
½ tsp. garlic powder
½ tsp. onion powder

Drain tofu and press for at least 15-30 minutes. Meanwhile, add the soy sauce, veg broth, garlic, vinegar, maple syrup, and 1 T. of cornstarch to a quart jar or ziplock bag and mix to form a marinade. Slice tofu into bite-sized cubes and add to marinade. Marinate for 15-30 minutes, frequently shaking to ensure even coverage. Drain marinade and reserve. Whisk the remaining cornstarch, paprika, and spices together and add mixture and the tofu to a large ziplock bag and shake until coated. Air fry tofu at 400° F for 10-15 minutes, shaking the basket frequently to prevent sticking. Alternatively, bake in a 400° F oven until browned. Heat reserved marinade in a small saucepan until thickened and pour on finished tofu or use as a dipping sauce.

SPICY AIR-FRIED GARLIC TOFU

Sauce

2 ½ T. low-sodium soy sauce
1 T. mirin
1 T. gochugaru Korean chile flakes

2 tsp. maple syrup
1 tsp. rice vinegar
1 tsp. cornstarch
½ c. water

12 oz. extra-firm tofu
3 green onions
5 cloves garlic, minced
1 red bell pepper

2 oz. shiitake mushrooms (opt.)
garnish: sliced green onion tops and/or sesame seeds

Whisk sauce ingredients together - set aside. Press tofu for 10-15 minutes to remove as much moisture as you can, then cut into equal-sized cubes. Brush cubes with a little soy sauce if desired, then air fry at 400° F. for 5-10 minutes, shaking the basket occasionally. Set aside when done. Finely chop the onions reserving some of the green tops for garnish, mince the garlic, and cut the red pepper into strips. Also clean and chop the mushrooms if you are using them. Add the veggies and sliced mushrooms (opt.) to a sauté pan with a little veg broth or water and sauté until softened. Stir in the sauce and fold in the cooked tofu cubes. Stir fry until the sauce has thickened. Garnish with sliced green onion tops and/or sesame seeds. Serve over rice.

Cooking is like love. It should be entered into with abandon or not at all.

- Harriet Van Horne

SPICY GENERAL TSO TOFU

Sauce

1 ½ T. minced garlic
1 T. minced ginger
½ c. low-sodium soy sauce
¼ c. rice vinegar
1 T. chile garlic paste
¼ c. water

1 T. mirin
1 T. tahini
3 T. sugar
1 pinch red pepper flakes (opt.)
1 T. cornstarch

Sauté garlic and ginger in ¼ cup soy sauce until softened. Add remaining soy sauce, rice vinegar, chile paste, water, mirin, tahini, sugar, and red pepper flakes (opt.) and stir until bubbly. In a small bowl, whisk 1 T. cornstarch to 1 T. water to make a slurry, add to sauce and stir to thicken.

Stir-Fry

14 oz. extra-firm tofu
1 (8 oz.) can pineapple chunks (juice & fruit divided)
1 T. low-sodium soy sauce
2 T. cornstarch
1 (12 oz.) pkg. frozen veggies (broccoli, carrots, water chestnuts)

4 oz. whole button mushrooms, sliced
½ c. cashews

Drain and press the tofu. Slice into 1" cubes and toss with pineapple juice and 1 T. soy sauce to marinade. Refrigerate 15-30 minutes while oven is heating up to 350° F. Drain marinade and toss tofu with 2 T. cornstarch. Place evenly on parchment lined cookie sheet and bake for 45 minutes or until crispy. Stir fry the frozen veggies, pineapple, mushrooms, and cashews in a small amount of water until crisp tender. Add tofu and sauce and stir to coat evenly.

A house is not a home unless it contains food and fire for the mind as well as the body.

- Benjamin Franklin

TOFU TACOS

- 16 oz. super-firm (high-protein) tofu
- 2 T. nutritional yeast
- 3 tsp. chili powder
- 1 tsp. garlic powder
- 1 tsp. smoked paprika
- ½ tsp. cumin
- ½ tsp. onion powder
- 3 T. low-sodium soy sauce
- 2 T. water
- 1 tsp. vegan Worcestershire
- ½ tsp. liquid smoke

Preheat oven to 350° F. Drain and pat the tofu dry, then crumble it into a large bowl. In a separate bowl, whisk all the dry ingredients together first, then mix in the wet ingredients to form a thick paste. Gently mix the paste into the tofu crumbles until they are evenly coated. Spread the crumbles in a single layer on a parchment-lined baking sheet. Bake for 30 minutes, stirring occasionally. Turn off the heat and let the crumbles continue to dry for an additional 15-30 minutes. Transfer the crumbles to a skillet and add 1 cup of water. Stir the taco meat over medium heat until most of the water has evaporated.

VEGAN MAPO TOFU

- 1 tsp. + 1 T. low-sodium soy sauce (divided)
- 1 tsp. tahini
- ½ tsp. Szechuan peppercorns (or black pepper)
- 5 oz. shiitake mushrooms, chopped
- 1 T. cornstarch
- 3 T. water
- 1 (16 oz.) block med-firm tofu
- 1 tsp. salt
- 4 cloves garlic
- 1 tsp. ginger
- 3 green onions (white & green parts separated)
- 1½ T. black bean paste
- 2 tsp. gochugaru Korean chili flakes
- 1 tsp. maple syrup
- 2 tsp. gochujang Korean Chile paste
- ½ c. frozen peas & carrots

Mix 1 teaspoon of soy sauce, the tahini, and black pepper together in a small bowl with the mushrooms, mixing well to ensure they are evenly coated - set aside. Whisk the cornstarch and water together to make a slurry - set aside. Carefully rinse and drain the tofu and pat dry. Then cut it into cubes. Add salt to a pot of water and bring to a boil. Gently add the tofu to the pot and simmer for 1 minute - remove from heat and set aside. Prep the veggies by mincing the garlic, ginger, and green onions. In a large sauté pan - sauté the mushrooms until softened. (Add a little water or broth as needed to prevent sticking.) Add the minced onion whites, garlic, and ginger, and then stir in the black bean paste and gochugaru. Sauté until veggies have softened and are aromatic. Mix well. Mix 1 cup of water, the remaining soy sauce, maple syrup, and gochujang, then add to the mushrooms. Mix well and bring to a boil. Reduce heat, add the peas & carrots, stir in the slurry, and gently fold in the drained tofu, making sure it gets coated with the sauce. Simmer for 5 minutes or until the sauce has thickened and slightly reduced. Top with sliced green onion tops and serve over rice.

Recipe Favorites

Multi Cooker Recipes

Multicooker Tips

Some of the recipes in this book I've made specifically for an Instant Pot. I realize not everyone owns an Instant Pot so rest assured they can be made on a stovetop also.

But if you DO have an Instant Pot, here are just a few tips and tricks you may find useful:

Sealing Rings Absorbing Odors & Flavors

1. Buy an extra sealing ring and use one for sweet & savory recipes and the other for spicier recipes.
2. Placing your sealing ring outside overnight will remove unwanted odors.
3. Store your Instant Pot with the lid upside down. This helps the sealing ring air out.
4. If your sealing ring gets too smelly, steam it with vinegar by adding 2 cups of white vinegar to your empty IP, attach the lid, and press STEAM. Cook for 2 minutes then rinse.

Cleaning

1. To keep the lip (*where the lid seats*) clean, use a damp foam brush
2. The entire lid is dishwasher safe on the top rack
3. Don't forget to clean the condensation cup periodically.

General

1. Always do the water test before you cook anything in your brand new IP. Instructions will be in your manual.
2. If the liner spins when stirring, use a large binder clip to hold it in place.
3. Be sure and try all the IP modes at least once.
4. Use the YOGURT setting (*if your model has one*) to proof dough. Place the included trivet in your IP liner, set your dough on a piece of parchment paper on the trivet, cover with lid and set your timer.
5. You can blend directly in your IP using an immersion blender.
6. If not using Natural Pressure Release (NPR), use a wooden spoon to release the steam and wear protective oven mitts, as the steam is very hot and can scald you.

MULTICOOKER RECIPES

15 BEAN SOUP

1 med. onion
1 green bell pepper
2 ribs celery
2 carrots
1 jalapeño (opt.)
1 (20 oz.) bag 15 bean soup mix
4 c. low-sodium vegetable broth
4 c. water
2 T. low-sodium soy sauce
3 cloves garlic, minced

1 (7 oz.) can roasted diced green chiles
¾ tsp. cumin
¾ tsp thyme
1 bay leaf
1 (15 oz.) can fire-roasted tomatoes
2 handfuls baby spinach
2 T. fresh lime juice

Dice all the fresh vegetables. Rinse the beans well, and add them to your Instant Pot. Throw away that little seasoning packet that comes in the beans, we won't be using it. Then add the broth, water, soy sauce, garlic, onion, peppers, chiles, celery, carrots, cumin, thyme, and bay leaf to your beans. Attach the lid and make sure it is sealed. Set your Instant Pot to SEALING, cook on MANUAL mode, high pressure, and 45 minutes. When finished cooking, allow to vent naturally. CAREFULLY remove the lid and stir in tomatoes, spinach, and lime juice. Mix well and check for seasoning. Add additional salt and pepper if needed.

BLACK BEAN SOUP

1 red onion
2 ribs celery
½ red bell pepper
4 cloves garlic, minced
2 tsp. Mexican oregano
2 tsp. chili powder
1 tsp. cumin
½ tsp. black pepper

2 c. low-sodium vegetable broth
2 c. water
2 c. dried black beans
1 (10 oz.) can Rotel tomatoes & green chiles
garnish: chopped green onions, cilantro, salsa, or lime wedges

Finely chop onion, celery, and bell pepper and add to an Instant Pot. Sauté veggies using SAUTÉ mode using a splash of water or veg broth to prevent sticking. Stir in garlic & spices and simmer just until they become aromatic - about 15-20 seconds. Press CANCEL to stop the sauté mode. Slowly add the vegetable broth and water and stir well. Rinse 2 cups of dried black beans, removing any debris, and add to pot. Stir to mix. Pour the Rotel tomatoes into the CENTER of the soup and DO NOT STIR. Attach the lid, make sure the vent is set to SEALING and set the timer for MANUAL mode for 30 minutes. When done, allow to naturally vent for 10 minutes before CAREFULLY releasing whatever steam is left. Remove 2 cups of the beans & veggies and blend until smooth. Add back into the soup and stir. Optional: Garnish with chopped green onions, cilantro, salsa, or lime wedges.

HOPPIN' JOHN

1 onion
1 carrot
2 ribs celery
2 c. dried black-eyed peas
1 c. rice
2 (15 oz.) cans diced tomatoes
4 c. low-sodium vegetable broth
1 c. water
3 cloves garlic, minced

2 tsp. thyme
1 tsp. onion powder
1 tsp. garlic powder
1 tsp. smoked paprika
1 bay leaf
½ bunch kale or similar greens
1 T. balsamic vinegar
Hot sauce to taste (opt.)

Dice onion, carrot, and celery and add to the Instant Pot. Rinse black-eyed peas and rice, and add to the Instant Pot. Add tomatoes, broth, and water. Add the garlic and spices. Stir to mix well and attach the lid. Seal. Cook on MANUAL for 20 minutes. Allow the steam to vent naturally for 15 minutes then carefully release any remaining pressure. Remove the tough ribs from the kale and shred the leaves. Stir kale into the beans and add balsamic to flavor. Taste for seasoning. Add hot sauce if desired.

IRISH COLCANNON

2 c. chopped green cabbage
3 oz. chopped kale
½ c. low-sodium vegetable broth
4 chopped green onions
4 cloves garlic, minced
½ c. water

3 lb. Yukon gold potatoes, quartered
1 T. white miso
¼ c. unsweetened almond milk (if needed)
salt & pepper to taste

Add cabbage and kale to the Instant Pot. Add broth and SAUTÉ until the kale is slightly wilted. Add onions and garlic, SAUTÉ 1 minute, and press CANCEL. Add water and potatoes. Attach lid, make sure vent is sealed, and cook on MANUAL for 7 minutes. After it finishes, let it sit for 10 minutes. CAREFULLY vent any remaining pressure and remove the lid. Add miso and mash, adding almond milk as needed. Add salt and pepper if needed and serve.

In the childhood memories of every good cook, there's a large kitchen, a warm stove, a simmering pot and a mom.
- Barbara Costikyan

PERFECT VEGGIE RICE

1 ½ c. whole grain brown rice
¼ c. diced onion
2 small carrots, diced
3 cloves garlic, minced

½ tsp. salt
1 tsp. yellow curry powder
2 c. low-sodium vegetable broth
1 c. frozen peas

Place rice in a fine sieve and rinse thoroughly, set aside to drain. Add diced onion and carrot to your Instant Pot. Add a few tablespoons of water or broth. Set your Instant Pot to SAUTÉ mode. Stir frequently until the onions start to turn translucent. Add garlic and rinsed rice - continue sautéing for another 30 seconds. Press the KEEP WARM/CANCEL button - and then add the salt, curry powder, and broth. Stir thoroughly and attach the lid, ensuring the valve is set to SEALING. Set Instant Pot to MANUAL or PRESSURE COOK mode and set timer for 24 minutes. Let Instant Pot naturally release pressure (NPR) for 10 minutes then carefully vent any remaining pressure. Add frozen peas and fluff rice with a fork.

SMOKY COWBOY BEANS

1 batch marinade from Smoky Maple Tofu Bacon, p. 66
4 oz. soy curls
1 onion
1 red bell pepper
1 (7 oz.) can roasted diced green chiles
3 tsp. minced garlic
1 (20 oz.) bag 15 bean soup mix with the seasoning packet

4 c. low-sodium vegetable broth
4 c. water
2 T. chili powder
1 (15 oz.) can fire-roasted tomatoes, drained
2 handfuls of chopped kale (or preferred greens)

Prepare the marinade, then cover the soy curls with it and ¼ cup water - set aside. Dice onion and bell pepper and add to your Instant Pot. Add the green chiles and SAUTÉ until veggies begin to soften, then add garlic. Add soy curls and any remaining marinade and stir. Sauté for 1 more minute then turn the Instant Pot OFF. Rinse and drain the beans and add to the pot along with veg broth and water. Add the chili powder and the seasoning packet from the soup mix and stir. Attach lid, set to SEALING, and cook on MANUAL for 45 minutes. Let pressure vent naturally for 10 minutes before CAREFULLY releasing any remaining pressure. Remove the lid and stir in tomatoes and greens. Stir until greens have wilted and serve.

SOUTHWESTERN SQUASH & CORN SOUP

Soup

1 Yukon gold potato
16 oz. yellow squash
1 c. diced onion
2 cloves garlic, minced
3 c. low-sodium vegetable broth
¾ tsp. salt
¼ tsp. white pepper

¼ tsp. cumin
2 (15 oz.) cans fire-roasted corn (or about 3 cups fresh or frozen)
1 (4 oz.) can roasted green chiles

Red Pepper Relish

½ red bell pepper
½ c. Italian parsley or cilantro
1 T. lemon (or lime) juice

1 tsp. maple syrup
¼ tsp. salt

Add diced potato, squash, onion, and garlic to Instant Pot. Add vegetable broth and season with salt, pepper, and cumin. Attach lid, set to SEALING, and cook on MANUAL for 7 minutes with a 10 minute natural pressure release. Carefully vent any remaining steam and remove the lid. Add 1 cup of corn and purée in batches in your blender or use an immersion blender. Blend until smooth. Return soup to Instant Pot and stir in remaining corn and green chiles. Heat through on WARM setting for 30 minutes. For the relish, dice the red pepper and mix in the remaining ingredients, then refrigerate until needed. Ladle soup into a bowl and top with a heaping teaspoon of relish for garnish.

SPANISH RICE

½ sm. onion
½ sm. red bell pepper
2 c. low-sodium vegetable broth
½ tsp. chili powder

¼ tsp. cumin
1 ½ c. white rice
1 c. salsa

Dice onion and bell pepper and add to your Instant Pot. Add just enough veg broth to the bottom to prevent sticking and using the SAUTÉ mode, sauté the veggies until soft. Add the veg broth and the spices and stir to combine. Rinse your rice well then add to your Instant Pot. Stir to combine. Add 1 cup of your favorite salsa to the center of the pot and DO NOT STIR. Attach the lid, set to SEALING, and cook on MANUAL mode, LOW PRESSURE, for 10 minutes. Allow pressure to release naturally for 5 minutes before carefully venting any remaining steam and removing the lid. Fluff rice with a fork and serve.

VEGAN REFRIED BEANS

½ onion
½ jalapeño
1 tsp. minced garlic

16 oz. dried pinto beans
½ tsp. cumin
½ tsp. salt

Roughly chop the onion and jalapeño and add to Instant Pot along with the garlic. Rinse beans thoroughly and add to Instant Pot. Add enough water to completely cover the beans by about 1 inch. Stir in cumin. Attach the lid, set it to SEALING, and cook on MANUAL mode for 45 minutes. When finished, allow the Instant Pot to vent naturally then carefully remove the lid. Remove the majority of the liquid by ladling it out into another container. Then mash beans to a creamy consistency using a potato masher, fork, or immersion blender. Beans will be slightly runny but will firm up when cooled. If additional liquid is needed, use the leftover bean liquid 1 T. at a time. Season with salt to taste.

A first-rate soup is more creative than a second-rate painting.

- Abraham H. Maslow

Recipe Favorites

Salads & Dressings

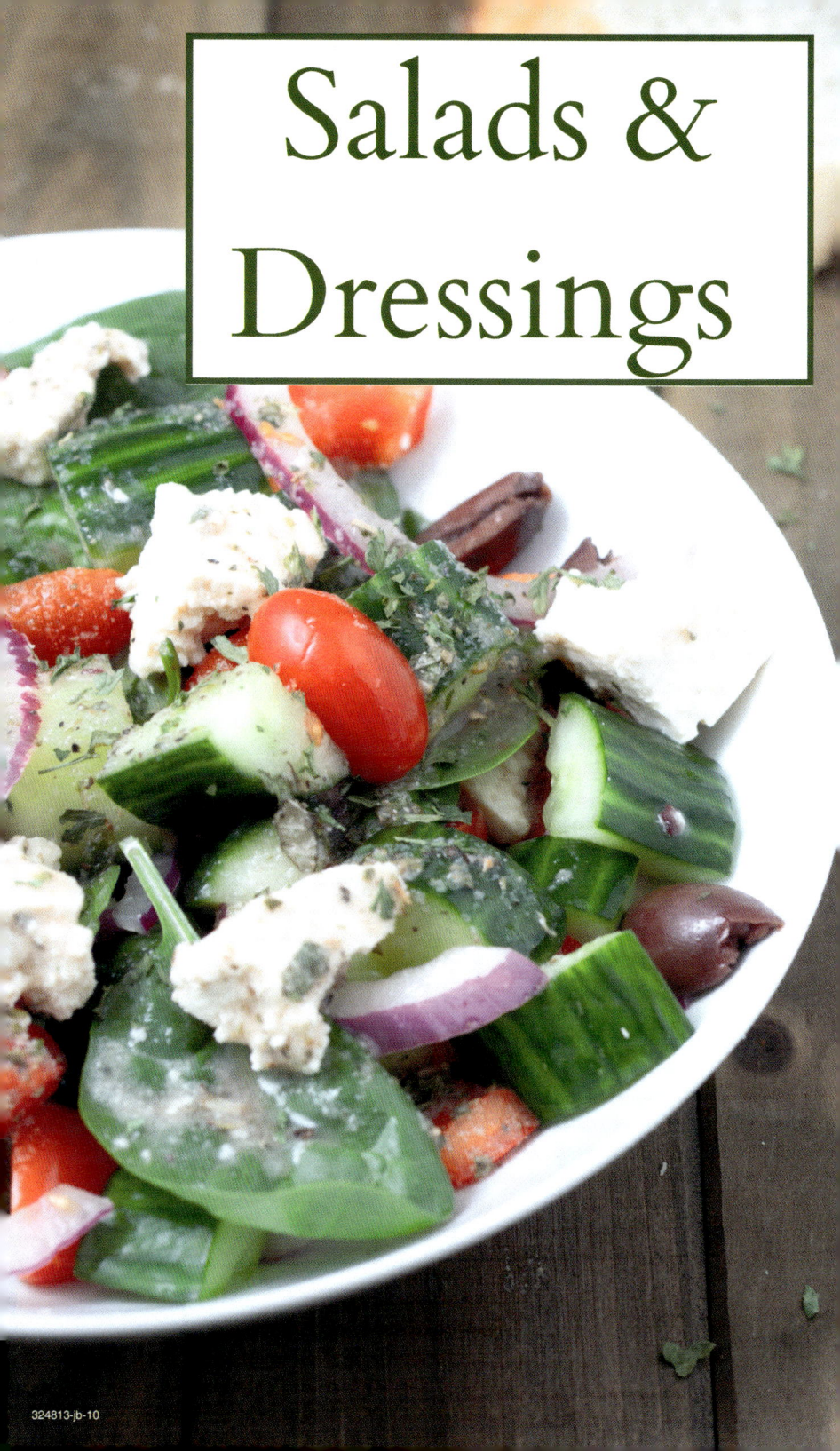

MY PANTRY

Fresh Produce (Fruit & Veggies)

The produce aisle is one on the first places I stop when going to the grocery store. Here are some of the more common fruits & veggies I have purchased since becoming plant-based.

- Apples
- Avocados
- Bananas
- Bell peppers (*all colors*)
- Berries
- Broccoli
- Brussels Sprouts
- Cabbage
- Cantaloupe
- Carrots
- Cauliflower
- Celery
- Cucumbers
- Garlic
- Green onions (*scallions*)
- Jalapenos (*green and red*)
- Kale, chard, other greens
- Leeks
- Lemons
- Lettuce (*iceberg, romaine, butter, arugula*)
- Limes
- Mushrooms
- Onions (*all colors*)
- Oranges
- Pineapple
- Potatoes (*gold, russet, red*)
- Spinach
- Squash (*zucchini, butternut, acorn*)
- Sweet potatoes
- Tomatillos
- Tomatoes
- Watermelon

SALADS & DRESSINGS

CREAMY VEGAN COLESLAW

1 (14 oz.) bag coleslaw mix
½ c. non-dairy plain yogurt
1 T. apple cider vinegar
1 T. Dijon mustard
1 T. brown sugar

1 ½ tsp. lemon juice
½ tsp. kosher salt
½ tsp. black pepper
¼ tsp. celery seeds

Add coleslaw mix to a large bowl. In a small bowl, whisk remaining dressing ingredients together until smooth and pour into coleslaw. Mix well and let rest for 1 hr. before serving.

FAT-FREE VEGAN POTATO SALAD

2 lbs. red potatoes (about 6)
¼ red onion
¼ red bell pepper
2 ribs celery
2-4 T. pickle relish
1 (15 oz.) can cannellini beans
3 T. lemon juice
1 T. red wine vinegar
1 T. white miso

1 T. Dijon mustard
1 T. dill pickle juice
1 T. maple syrup
½ tsp. garlic powder
½ tsp. black pepper
½ tsp. celery seed
¼ tsp. onion powder
¼ tsp. salt
garnish: paprika (opt.)

Wash and scrub the potatoes. INSTANT POT: Add your steamer trivet to your Instant Pot, the potatoes, and 1 ½ cups of water. Set to SEALING, then cook on MANUAL at high pressure for 4 minutes. Let it naturally vent when finished. STOVE TOP: Add the potatoes to a large pan and cover with water. Boil until just fork tender - 5-10 minutes. Remove potatoes, drain, and set aside in the refrigerator to cool while preparing salad and dressing. Finely chop onion, red bell pepper, and celery and add to a large bowl along with the pickle relish. Mix thoroughly. For the dressing, drain and rinse the beans and add them to your blender along with all the remaining ingredients. Blend on high until smooth. Add 1 T. water at a time to thin if needed. Chop the cooled potatoes and carefully mix them with the salad ingredients. Fold in at least 1 cup of the dressing (or as much as you like). Mix carefully. Chill for at least 30 minutes and serve. Garnish with a dusting of paprika if desired.

OIL-FREE PASTA SALAD

Dressing

1 (15 oz.) can cannellini beans
3 T. lemon juice
1 T. red wine vinegar
1 T. white miso
1 T. dill pickle juice
1 T. spicy brown mustard

½ tsp. garlic powder
½ tsp. black pepper
¼ tsp. fresh dill
¼ tsp. onion powder
¼ tsp. salt

Add all dressing ingredients to your blender, including the liquid from the can of beans and blend on high until smooth. It may look a little thin but the pasta will soak it up.

Pasta Salad

4 c. pasta
2 ribs celery
3 green onions
½ red bell pepper

1-2 radishes
2 T. pimento
2 T. sweet pickle relish

Cook pasta according to package instructions. Drain and rinse well when finished and set aside. Chop all veggies and add to a large bowl. Gently toss pasta and all remaining ingredients together and fold in dressing. Gently stir until everything is well-coated. Cover and chill in the refrigerator for at least 1-2 hrs. before serving.

OIL-FREE VEGAN CAESAR DRESSING

¼ c. raw cashews
¾ c. riced cauliflower
¾ c. water
3 T. lemon juice
2 T. nutritional yeast
3 tsp. minced garlic

3 tsp. Dijon mustard
2 tsp. capers
1 tsp. vegan Worcestershire sauce
1 tsp. white miso
Black pepper to taste

Soak the cashews in hot water for at least 20 minutes. Drain and add to the blender along with all the remaining ingredients. Process until smooth and creamy, scraping down the sides as needed. Store in a glass cruet or jar in the refrigerator for 3-5 days.

VEGAN GREEK SALAD WITH TOFU FETA

Greek Salad

- 2 English cucumbers
- 1 red bell pepper
- ½ red onion
- 1 pt. cherry tomatoes
- 1 (15 oz.) can chickpeas
- handful baby spinach
- ¼ c. kalamata olives, sliced (opt.)

Chop cucumbers and bell pepper into bite-sized pieces and place in a large salad bowl. Thinly slice the onion, cut the cherry tomatoes in half, and mix them into the salad. Drain the liquid from the can of chickpeas and save (we'll need ¼ cup for the dressing). Add the chickpeas and spinach to the bowl. Complete steps for dressing and feta, adding the dressing to the bowl and tossing to coat. Add as little or as much feta as desired. Garnish with sliced olives, as desired.

Oil-Free Greek Dressing

- ⅓ c. red wine vinegar
- ¼ c. aquafaba (liquid from a can of chickpeas)
- ½ tsp. Dijon mustard
- ¾ tsp. dried basil
- ¾ tsp. oregano
- ¾ tsp. garlic powder
- ½ tsp. onion powder
- ¼ tsp. salt
- ¼ tsp. black pepper
- 1 T. chopped kalamata olives (opt.)

Mix all ingredients together. Whisk or shake in a closed container until thoroughly mixed.

Tofu Feta

- 12 oz. extra firm tofu
- ¼ c. red wine vinegar
- 2 T. lemon juice
- 2 T. nutritional yeast
- 1 T. white miso
- 1 tsp. oregano
- ½ tsp. garlic powder
- ¼ tsp. salt

Drain and press the tofu and crumble into bite-sized pieces. Mix the remaining ingredients and pour over the crumbled tofu in a shallow bowl. Mix, cover, and refrigerate until needed.

VEGAN RANCH DRESSING

- 1 c. raw cashews
- 1 c. unsweetened almond milk
- 2 T. lemon juice
- 1 tsp. apple cider vinegar
- 1 tsp. white miso
- 1 tsp. garlic powder
- 1 tsp. onion powder
- 1 tsp. dried parsley
- ¾ tsp. ground dill
- ½ tsp. salt

Soak cashews in hot water for at least 1 hour. Drain well and add to blender along with remaining ingredients. Blend on high until smooth and creamy.

VEGAN THOUSAND ISLAND DRESSING

14 oz. silken tofu
3 T. + 1 tsp. lemon juice
1 T. apple cider vinegar
1 T. dill pickle juice
1 T. low-sodium soy sauce
¾ tsp. yellow mustard
½ tsp. garlic powder
½ tsp. onion powder
¼ tsp. salt
3 T. ketchup
½ c. dill pickle relish

Drain the tofu and add it to a blender. Add all remaining ingredients except for the ketchup and relish. Process until smooth. Empty into a small bowl and stir in ketchup and relish. Refrigerate until ready to use.

Give a man a fish and you feed him for a day. Teach him how to fish and you feed him for a lifetime.

- Lao Tzu

Sandwiches & Wraps

Vegan Substitutions for Dairy & Eggs

I was never a fan of drinking milk or eating eggs, even before I became plant based. Sure, I had cereal and milk when I was young, but that's about it. But they do play an important part in cooking, so it's good to know substitutes you can use.

Fortunately, there is a wide variety of plant based dairy products available today including plant based butter, sour cream, yogurt, egg replacers, cheese, and of course milk, all of which can be used to create vegan meals.

However, be careful, many of these products are still highly processed, so whenever I can, I make my own. Several of those recipes are in this book, like my cheese sauce and even a sour cream.

For replacing 1 egg in baking, you can use any of the following:

- 1 T. ground flaxseed + 3 T. water
- 2 T. arrowroot + 3 T. water
- 2 T. cornstarch + 3 T. water
- 3 T. peanut butter
- 3 T. chickpea flour + 3 T. water
- 3T. aquafaba (juice from can of chickpeas)
- 1 T. powdered egg replacer + 2 T. water
- 1/2 mashed banana
- 1 T. chia seed + 1/3 c. water
- 1/4 c. applesauce
- 1/4 c. silken tofu
- 1/4 c. vegan yogurt

SANDWICHES & WRAPS

CHICKPEA SALAD (VEGAN TUNA SALAD)

½ c. raw cashews
½ c. water
1 (15 oz.) can chickpeas
  (garbanzo beans)
½ c. minced red onion
1 rib celery
1 sm. carrot

3 T. lemon juice
2 T. dill pickle relish
1 T. yellow mustard
2 tsp. apple cider vinegar
1 tsp. nutritional yeast
1 tsp. low-sodium soy sauce
½ tsp. garlic powder

Add the cashews and water to your blender to let them soak. Rinse and drain chickpeas and then mash them in a large bowl using a potato masher or fork. Mince the onion, celery, and carrot and stir into the chickpeas. Add all the remaining liquid ingredients to the blender with the cashews and pulse until smooth. Fold the dressing into the salad and mix well.

My idea of heaven is a great big baked potato and someone to share it with.

- Oprah Winfrey

ITALIAN SAUSAGE AND PEPPERS

Italian Sausage

½ c. white beans
1 c. low-sodium vegetable broth
2 T. low-sodium soy sauce
1 T. tomato paste
1¼ c. vital wheat gluten
¼ c. nutritional yeast
1½ tsp. fennel seed
1 tsp. onion powder

1 tsp. garlic powder
1 tsp. oregano
½ tsp. smoked paprika
½ tsp. thyme
½ tsp. salt
¼ tsp. black pepper
¼ tsp. chipotle chili powder
¼ tsp. red chile flakes

Drain the beans and add ½ cup to your blender (save remaining beans). Add veg broth, soy sauce, and tomato paste to beans and blend until smooth, and set aside. In a large bowl, mix vital wheat gluten, nutritional yeast, and all the spices. Pour wet ingredients into dry and mix just until a soft dough is formed. Cut into 4 equal pieces. Roll each piece into a sausage-shaped log, roll loosely in parchment paper, then foil, and twist ends to seal. Steam in a steamer basket or Instant Pot using trivet and STEAM function for 40 minutes. Allow to cool before using.

Pasta Dinner

2 c. pasta
2 onions
1 green bell pepper
1 red bell pepper
2-3 Italian sausages
3 cloves garlic, minced

1 (14 oz.) can diced tomatoes
1-2 T. tomato paste
Remaining white beans (opt.)
½ tsp. oregano
½ tsp. basil
½ tsp. red wine vinegar

Prepare 2 cups of your favorite pasta and then drain. Cut onions and peppers into strips. Cut 2-3 of the sausages into ½" pieces. Sauté the onions and peppers in a large pan or Dutch oven, using a little water to prevent sticking. Add minced garlic and stir. Add tomatoes, tomato paste, leftover beans (opt.), and remaining seasonings and vinegar. Cook until heated through and then add sausage pieces and pasta. Simmer for 4-5 minutes then serve.

You've got to go out on a limb sometimes because that's where the fruit is.

- Will Rogers

MUSHROOM REUBEN

Marinade

¼ c. low-sodium soy sauce
¼ c. low-sodium vegetable broth
1 T. maple syrup
1 T. vegan Worcestershire sauce
1 T. brown mustard

1 tsp. liquid smoke
1 tsp. smoked paprika
1 tsp. onion powder
½ tsp. garlic powder
½ tsp. caraway seeds
¼ tsp. black pepper

Sandwich

3 lg. (8 oz.) portobello mushroom caps
Buns or bread of your choice
Your favorite sauerkraut

Vegan 1000 Island Dressing, p. 62
Amazing Vegan Cheese Sauce, p. 71 (opt.)

If cheese sauce is desired, prepare it first, then prepare the 1000 Island dressing. Prepare marinade by combining all marinade ingredients and mixing well. Slice mushrooms and place in a shallow dish. Cover with the marinade and plastic wrap. Marinate for at least 1 hour - stirring or shaking occasionally. Simmer mushrooms with marinade in a large skillet until mushrooms have reduced in size and most of the marinade has evaporated. Toast bread if desired. To assemble, spread 1000 Island dressing on one piece of bread, top with mushrooms, sauerkraut, cheese sauce, and the remaining piece of bread.

No man is lonely eating spaghetti; it requires so much attention.

- Christopher Morley

PORTOBELLO FRENCH DIP

Au Jus

1 ¾ c. low-sodium vegetable broth
2 T. low-sodium soy sauce
1 T. vegan Worcestershire sauce
2 tsp. molasses
¼ tsp. liquid smoke
1 T. cornstarch or arrowroot powder

Sandwich

1 lg. sweet onion
2 med. bell peppers
¼ tsp. salt
2 tsp. minced garlic
16 oz. portobello mushroom caps
1 tsp. Italian seasoning
buns or bread of your choice

In a small bowl, whisk together the au jus ingredients and set aside. Slice onion and peppers into thin rings/strips and add to a large skillet, sprinkle with salt. Cook onions and peppers on med heat, stirring frequently, until they begin to soften - use 1-2 T. veg broth or water to prevent sticking. Add garlic and stir to combine. Cut mushrooms into ¼" thick slices. Add mushrooms to skillet and sauté until they begin to shrink in size and release their liquid. Add Italian seasoning and mix well. When the liquid from the mushroom has almost evaporated, slowly pour in the au jus. Simmer mushrooms until the sauce slightly thickens. Season with salt and pepper. Assemble sandwiches on the bread of your choice. Serve with au jus on the side for dipping.

SMOKY MAPLE TOFU BACON

1 (14 oz.) block extra-firm tofu
¼ c. low-sodium soy sauce
2 T. maple syrup
1 T. nutritional yeast
2 tsp. liquid smoke
1 tsp. onion powder
½ tsp. garlic powder

Drain the tofu, wrap the block in paper towels, and press under something heavy to remove as much moisture as possible. Let press for 15 minutes. Carefully slice tofu lengthwise into ⅛" slices. Whisk all remaining ingredients together in a small bowl to make the marinade. Lay the slices of tofu flat in a large pan or dish and cover with marinade. Let the tofu marinate for at least 15 minutes, preferably 30 minutes to 1 hr. To broil: Place the tofu slices on a foil-lined baking sheet and place them under your broiler. Turn occasionally to brown both sides. Note: Do not use parchment paper. To pan fry: Place the slices in a non-stick skillet and cook on med-high heat until browned, flipping occasionally.

SMOKY VEGAN CARROT DOGS ★

6-8 carrots
¼ c. low-sodium soy sauce
¼ c. apple cider vinegar
¼ c. low-sodium vegetable broth
2 T. maple syrup
1 T. liquid smoke
1 tsp. yellow mustard
1 tsp. garlic
1 tsp. pickled jalapeño juice
½ tsp. onion powder

Cut and peel carrots to make them "bun length." Boil carrots in water until just fork tender, about 10-15 minutes. Drain carrots, rinse with cold water, and drain again. Place carrots in a ziplock freezer bag. Whisk all marinade ingredients together and pour into bag with carrots. Marinate for 4-6 hrs., turning over occasionally. Grill carrots on an open grill, basting occasionally. Grill to heat all the way through and to get some blackened grill marks on each side.

SPICY SOUTHWESTERN BLACK BEAN BURGER 🌶

½ c. old-fashioned rolled oats
1 (15 oz.) can black beans
1 (15 oz.) can kidney beans
¼ c. cornmeal
½ c. salsa
1 chipotle pepper with adobo sauce
2 tsp. cumin
½ tsp. onion powder
½ tsp. garlic powder
¼ tsp. salt

Preheat oven to 350° F. Using a food processor, grind oats into flour and set aside. Drain beans into a colander and rinse well. Spread beans onto a cookie sheet and dry them as best you can. Bake for 20 minutes. Add beans, oats, cornmeal, salsa, chipotle pepper, and remaining spices together in a food processor and process until smooth, scraping down sides as necessary. Form into 5 patties and allow them to set in the refrigerator for at least 1 hour. Grill burgers as usual and garnish with your favorite toppings.

Too much food spoils the appetite, and too much talk becomes worthless.

- Chinese Proverb

VEGAN BANH MI SANDWICH

Pickled Slaw

1 c. shredded carrots
1 c. shredded daikon radish (or jicama)
⅔ c. rice vinegar
⅓ c. hot water

Peel carrots and daikon radish. Carefully shred or julienne about 1 cup each of the carrot and daikon. Place veggies in a glass bowl and add vinegar and water. Stir occasionally and set aside. Drain before using.

Tofu Remoulade

8 oz. silken tofu
1 T. lemon juice
1 T. sriracha (or to taste)
2 tsp. hoisin sauce
1 tsp. apple cider vinegar
1 clove garlic, minced
¼ tsp. salt

Place all the ingredients into a blender and blend until smooth, scraping down sides as necessary

Sandwich

¼ c. sliced onions
16 oz. portobello mushrooms
¼ c. low-sodium soy sauce
2 T. maple syrup
½ tsp. liquid smoke
2 (6 inch) French baguettes
sliced cucumber, jalapeños, or cilantro for garnish

Slice onion and gently sauté in 1-2 T. water until softened. Slice the portobellos thinly and add to pan. Gently sauté until softened and they begin to release their own liquid. Add soy sauce, maple syrup, and liquid smoke and stir well. Simmer until most of the liquid has cooked off and evaporated. Slice each baguette lengthwise and slather with the tofu remoulade. Toast 5 minutes at 350° F. Pile high with generous amounts of mushrooms, drained slaw, and your choice of garnishes.

The only time to eat diet food is while you are waiting for the steak to cook.

- Julia Child

VEGAN BEER BRATS

½ c. cannellini beans
1 ¼ c. vital wheat gluten
¼ c. nutritional yeast
1 tsp. fennel seeds
1 tsp. garlic powder
1 tsp. onion powder
1 tsp. rubbed sage
½ tsp. mustard powder

½ tsp. smoked paprika
½ tsp. black pepper
½ tsp. salt
¼ tsp. allspice
1 T. white miso
2 T. low-sodium soy sauce
1 c. beer
¼ tsp. liquid smoke

Rinse and drain cannellini beans and set aside. Whisk all dry ingredients together in a large bowl until thoroughly combined. In a separate bowl, blend all wet ingredients--including the cannellini beans--until thoroughly mixed and smooth. Add wet ingredients to dry and mix to form a loose dough. Cover and let rest while preparing foil sheets and steamer. Add 1-2 inches of water to steamer and turn it on. Pull off 5 sheets of aluminum foil, making them square. Cut dough into 5 equal pieces and shape into logs 5-6" long. Roll each log in foil and twist edges to seal. (You can use parchment paper in between the brats and the foil if you wish.) Steam for 45 minutes. Let rest 30 minutes. Enjoy as is, dry fry in a pan, or grill for additional browning.

At a dinner-party one should eat wisely but not too well, and talk well but not too wisely.

- W. Somerset Maugham

VEGAN GYROS WITH TZATZIKI SAUCE

Tzatziki Sauce

- 12 oz. extra-firm tofu
- 3 cloves garlic, minced
- 1 English cucumber
- 3 T. lemon juice
- 1 T. apple cider vinegar
- 1 T. fresh dill
- ½ tsp. salt

Drain tofu and pat dry, slice into smaller cubes, and add to blender. Add remaining sauce ingredients to blender and process until smooth, stopping to scrape down the sides if necessary. Pour into a bowl and set in the fridge until ready to serve.

Mushroom Gyros

- 16 oz. portobello mushrooms, sliced
- ¼ c. low-sodium soy sauce
- 2 T. maple syrup
- 2 T. water
- 1 tsp. oregano
- ½ tsp. garlic powder
- ½ tsp. onion powder
- ½ tsp. cumin
- ½ tsp. liquid smoke
- ¼ tsp. rosemary
- ¼ tsp. black pepper
- Basic Oil-Free Hummus, p. 11
- 4-5 pitas
- Garnishes: English cucumber, sliced; cherry tomatoes, sliced; red onion, sliced; romaine lettuce, shredded.

Place mushrooms in a large skillet. Whisk the remaining marinade ingredients together in a small cup or bowl until smooth and pour over the mushrooms. Cook mushrooms over medium heat until reduced in size and most of the marinade has cooked off. (Optional: Place mushrooms under the broiler for extra crispness.) Using your favorite pita (or wrap) spread some of your favorite hummus down the middle of each pita and layer on fresh veggies and other garnishes. Drizzle with tzatziki sauce. Wrap and enjoy!

Strange to see how a good dinner and feasting reconciles everybody.

- Samuel Pepys

Sauces & Gravy

Understanding Calorie Density

Many of us who follow a whole-food, plant-based diet use the knowledge of calorie density to our advantage.

Calorie density is simply the amount of calories in a certain food, as some foods have a lot more calories packed in than others.

For example, olive oil has 4,000 calories per pound, whereas spinach has just 100 calories per pound. We try to eat foods that are ABOVE the green line, as they have the least calorie density.

It is said the average person eats about 4 pounds of food a day, so you can see how 2400 calories a day can be achieved eating foods that are 600 calories or less per pound. But if we eat a lot of processed junk food instead, at 2300 calories per pounds, we could easily put away 9000 calories in a day.

In short, foods that are colored green in the chart are your friends. If they are yellow – be careful. And if they are red – stop and ask yourself if they are *really* necessary.

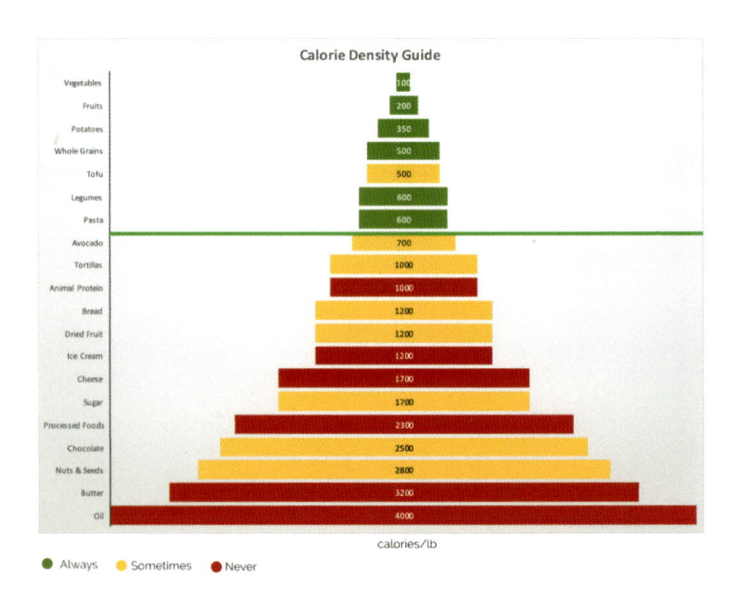

Calorie Density Guide

Food	calories/lb
Vegetables	100
Fruits	200
Potatoes	350
Whole Grains	500
Tofu	500
Legumes	600
Pasta	600
Avocado	700
Tortillas	1000
Animal Protein	1000
Bread	1200
Dried Fruit	1200
Ice Cream	1200
Cheese	1700
Sugar	1700
Processed Foods	2300
Chocolate	2500
Nuts & Seeds	2800
Butter	3200
Oil	4000

● Always ● Sometimes ● Never

SAUCES & GRAVY

AMAZING VEGAN CHEESE SAUCE

16 oz. Yukon gold potatoes
1 carrot
½ c. water, reserved from cooking vegetables
6 T. nutritional yeast
2 T. lemon juice

1 tsp. apple cider vinegar
1 tsp. salt
½ tsp. onion powder
½ tsp. garlic powder
½ tsp. yellow mustard
¼ tsp. turmeric

Wash and scrub potatoes and carrot, peel if desired, chop into uniform pieces and boil for 10 minutes. Let rest for 5 minutes and then with a slotted spoon, transfer the veggies to your blender. Add ½ cup of the veggie water and pulse to mix. Add remaining ingredients and blend until smooth and creamy.

BEST EVER FAT-FREE VEGAN GRAVY

¼ c. whole wheat flour
2 T. nutritional yeast
1 tsp. onion powder
½ tsp. garlic powder
½ tsp. black pepper

2 c. low-sodium vegetable broth
2 T. low-sodium soy sauce
½ tsp. yellow mustard
½ tsp. browning sauce (opt.)

Toast dry ingredients in a small saucepan over low heat until aromatic. Slowly add veg broth, whisking to remove any clumps. Add soy sauce, mustard, and browning sauce and stir to combine. Simmer on med-low heat until bubbly and thickened.

Good apple pies are a considerable part of our domestic happiness.

- Jane Austen

BOLOGNESE SAUCE

The "Meat"

2 c. riced cauliflower
1 c. diced mushrooms
¼ c. walnuts, finely chopped
2 T. low-sodium soy sauce
1 T. Italian seasoning
2 tsp. paprika

Preheat oven to 350° F. Add 2 cups of riced cauliflower to a large bowl. Or - finely chop about 2 cups of fresh cauliflower and add to bowl. Add diced mushrooms, walnuts, soy sauce, Italian seasoning, and paprika. Stir well to combine. Spread mixture onto a parchment-lined baking sheet and bake for 30 minutes. Stir once or twice during baking.

"Bolognese Sauce"

1 med. onion
1 rib celery
1 lg. carrot
4 cloves garlic, minced
1 c. white wine
1 (28 oz.) can San Marzano tomatoes
1 (6 oz.) can tomato paste
1 c. unsweetened almond milk
¼ c. fresh basil
1 T. oregano
1 tsp. rubbed sage
¼ tsp. salt
¼ tsp. black pepper
¼ tsp. red pepper flakes
¼ tsp. nutmeg

Finely dice the onion, celery, and carrot, and then sauté them in a few tablespoons of veg broth (or water) until softened. Stir in garlic and simmer until fragrant - about 30 seconds. Add wine and stir to deglaze the pan. Be sure to scrape up any burnt bits that may be stuck to the bottom of the pan. Add tomatoes, tomato paste, and almond milk and mix well. Add all the seasonings and mix well. Simmer uncovered for 20-30 minutes to allow flavors to come together. Stir in the "meat" you prepared earlier. Continue simmering until it thickens. Adjust for seasonings and serve over your favorite pasta.

Tell me what you eat and I will tell you what you are.
- Anthelme Brillat-Savarin

OIL-FREE MARINARA SAUCE

⅓ c. onion
⅓ c. red bell pepper
⅓ c. mushrooms
2 cloves garlic, minced
½ c. red wine
1 (15 oz.) can no-salt tomatoes
1 (15 oz.) can fire-roasted tomatoes

1 (6 oz.) can tomato paste
1 tsp. oregano
1 tsp. basil
1 tsp. parsley
¼ tsp. red wine vinegar
1 tsp. brown sugar (opt.)

Finely dice the onion and bell pepper to a uniform size. Sauté them together in a saucepan, just until they soften. Use a tablespoon or two of veg broth or water to prevent sticking if needed. Slice the mushrooms, add to pan, and continue cooking until they have reduced in size and released their liquid. Stir in the minced garlic and continue simmering for 1 minute or until fragrant. Add the wine and stir to combine. Cook for 1-2 minutes. The wine adds a very elegant flavor to the sauce but can be replaced with veg broth if necessary. Add the tomatoes and tomato paste and mix thoroughly. Add the remaining seasonings and simmer uncovered on low heat for about 30 minutes. The brown sugar is optional but helps reduce the overall acidity. If the sauce is too chunky for your liking - you can use an immersion blender or blend a cup or two in a blender, to get the consistency you like.

ULTIMATE FAT-FREE PIZZA SAUCE

1 (6 oz.) can tomato paste
¾ c. hot water
3 cloves garlic, minced
1 tsp. brown sugar
¾ tsp. onion powder
½ tsp. oregano

½ tsp. basil
¼ tsp. Italian seasoning
¼ tsp. black pepper
¼ tsp. red wine vinegar
pinch of red pepper flakes or cayenne

Add the tomato paste to a medium-sized bowl. Add hot water and whisk until smooth. Add the remaining ingredients, one at a time, while constantly stirring. Cover and let sit for at least 30 minutes for the flavors to come together.

Kissing don't last; cookery do!

- George Meredith

VEGAN COUNTRY SAUSAGE GRAVY

Vegan Sausage

1 ½ c. riced cauliflower
4 oz. mushrooms
1 c. walnuts
2 T. low-sodium soy sauce
1 tsp. molasses
1 tsp. maple syrup
¼ tsp. liquid smoke

2 T. nutritional yeast
1 ½ tsp. rubbed sage
½ tsp. black pepper
½ tsp. garlic powder
¼ tsp. nutmeg
½ tsp. thyme

Preheat oven to 350° F. Finely chop mushrooms and walnuts to uniform size. Mix together in a bowl with the riced cauliflower and add soy sauce, molasses, maple syrup, and liquid smoke. Add remaining ingredients and mix well. Turn out evenly onto parchment lined baking sheet and bake for 30 minutes. After 30 minutes, flip/mix with a spatula and continue baking for an additional 15 minutes.

Gravy

½ c. flour
1 T. nutritional yeast
1 tsp. rubbed sage
½ tsp. salt

½ tsp. black pepper
⅛ tsp. thyme
3-4 c. unsweetened almond milk

Mix all dry ingredients in a skillet and toast over med heat for a few minutes. Increase heat to med-high and slowly stir in almond milk, whisking continuously to break up any clumps. Once it begins to bubble, lower the heat and add the sausage crumbles. Stir until it has thickened to desired consistency. Add more milk to thin if necessary.

VEGAN GARLIC AIOLI SAUCE

1 c. raw cashews
1 (15 oz.) can white beans
½ c. water
3 cloves garlic, minced

2 T. lemon juice
1 T. nutritional yeast
½ tsp. salt

Soak cashews in enough water to cover for 1-2 hrs., then drain. Drain the beans also and then add all the ingredients to a blender and process until smooth and creamy.

VEGAN MUSHROOM GRAVY

½ diced onion
4 cloves garlic, minced
2 T. white wine
16 oz. mushrooms
2 T. low-sodium soy sauce
¼ c. whole wheat flour
1 T. nutritional yeast
½ tsp. dried thyme
½ tsp. rubbed sage
½ tsp. dried rosemary
2 ¼ c. low-sodium vegetable broth
½ tsp. gravy browning sauce (opt.)
1-2 drops liquid smoke (opt.)

Sauté onion and garlic in the wine (or veg broth/water) until softened. Add sliced mushrooms and soy sauce and cook until most of the liquid has evaporated. In a separate bowl, mix flour, nutritional yeast, and herbs. Alternate adding a little of the flour mixture to the mushroom mixture and then a little broth while stirring. Continue until you have added all of the flour and broth. If using the optional browning sauce and liquid smoke - add them as well. Mix well as mixture thickens.

VEGAN PARMESAN

¾ c. raw cashews
3 T. nutritional yeast
¾ tsp. salt
¼ tsp. garlic powder

Add all ingredients to a food processor or chopper and grind to desired consistency.

But civilized men cannot live without cooks.
- Owen Meredith

Recipe Favorites

Side Dishes

MY PANTRY

Beans & Legumes

It's no surprise that in areas of the world where people live naturally long and healthy lives well into their 90s and 100s (*The Blue Zones*), one food they consume daily is beans, specifically, about 1 cup of beans per day.

Dried beans are the most economical but take the most time to prepare. An electric pressure cooker can help with this. But don't discount canned beans as they are readily available, quick to cook, and can easily be rinsed and drained, lowering the sodium levels.

Eating beans has numerous health benefits including:

1. Full of protein & fiber
2. Rich in polyphenols (*antioxidants*)
3. Reduces risk of heart disease
4. Reduces risk of cancer
5. Stabilizes blood sugar
6. Controls appetite
7. Improves gut health

Some of my pantry favorites are:

- Bean Soup Mix
- Black Beans
- Black Eyed Peas
- Chickpeas (Garbanzo)
- Great Northern Beans
- Kidney Beans
- Lentils (red & green)
- Navy Beans
- Peas
- Pinto Beans
- Refried Beans
- White Beans

SIDE DISHES

BEST DANG BBQ BAKED BEANS

3 c. dried great northern beans
2 c. low-sodium vegetable broth
1 diced onion
4 cloves garlic, minced
1 diced green bell pepper
½ jalapeño, minced
1 tsp. salt

1 (6 oz.) can tomato paste
¼ c. molasses
¼ c. dark brown sugar
1 T. yellow mustard
1 tsp. apple cider vinegar
¼ tsp. chipotle chili powder
¼ tsp. black pepper

Soak beans overnight covered in water. Drain and rinse the beans the next morning. Add enough water to cover and bring to a boil. As soon as the beans begin to boil, remove from heat and cover. Let rest 30 minutes. Reserving 2 cups of the bean water, drain and rinse the beans. Add beans back into pot, with 2 cups of the bean water. Add vegetable broth, onion, garlic, peppers, and salt. Bring to a boil again and simmer on low for 1 hr. Add mixture to crock pot along with all the remaining ingredients and slow cook on low 4-6 hrs. or until tender.

SAVORY SUCCOTASH

½ yellow onion
2 cloves garlic, minced
1 red bell pepper, diced
1 tomato
1 (4 oz.) can diced green chiles
1 zucchini, peeled and diced
½ c. low-sodium vegetable broth

10 oz. frozen lima beans
1 (15 oz.) can corn
2 tsp. white miso
pinch of freshly ground black pepper
3 T. fresh parsley for garnish

Sauté onion & a pinch of salt until softened, about 5 minutes, adding a tablespoon of water or veg broth if needed. Stir in garlic and sauté for 1 minute. Add diced red bell pepper and cook for 3-4 minutes. Add diced tomato and green chiles, and mix well. Add zucchini and ¼ cup broth, and cook for 5 minutes or until tender. Rinse lima beans well, drain, and add to the pan. Drain corn and add to the mix. Stir in miso and a few grinds of black pepper. Taste for seasoning, and adjust if needed. Garnish with fresh parsley and serve.

SOUTHERN VEGAN GREEN BEANS

Mushroom Bacon

8 oz. baby bella mushrooms
¼ c. low-sodium soy sauce
2 T. maple syrup
2 T. water
½ tsp. garlic powder

½ tsp. onion powder
½ tsp. cumin
½ tsp. liquid smoke
¼ tsp. black pepper

Clean and slice mushrooms, and add to a large skillet. Whisk the remaining ingredients and pour over the mushrooms. Cook until mushrooms have reduced in size. Drain and save the marinade.

Main Dish

2 lbs. green beans (fresh or frozen)
1 lg. onion
24 oz. baby gold potatoes
2 c. low-sodium vegetable broth
2 c. water

leftover marinade from the mushroom bacon
½ tsp. garlic powder
½ tsp. onion powder
½ tsp. black pepper
¼ tsp. salt

Rinse the green beans, snap off both ends, and remove any strings if using fresh and set aside. In a large soup pan, dice and sauté a large onion until softened. Add the beans, potatoes, veg broth, water, and any leftover marinade from the bacon. Add remaining seasonings, stir, and cover. Bring beans to a boil, then reduce heat to a simmer. Cook for 1 hour then remove lid. Add bacon and stir.

We're gonna kick it up a notch!

- Emeril Lagasse

STUFFED MUSHROOMS ★

12 med. baby bella mushrooms
1 c. low-sodium vegetable broth
½ c. rice
¼ c. Vegan Parmesan, p. 75
½ c. diced white onion
1 rib celery, diced
2 cloves garlic, minced

1 tsp. rosemary
1 tsp. rubbed sage
¼ tsp. thyme
¼ tsp salt
¼ tsp. black pepper
¼ c. dried cranberries
2 tsp. balsamic vinegar

Preheat oven to 350° F. Clean mushrooms, remove stems, and set aside. Use a small spoon to make an opening large enough for stuffing in each cap. Bake caps in oven for 10 minutes, then set aside. Bring veg broth to a boil and then turn off the heat. Add thoroughly rinsed rice and cover with a lid. Allow rice to steep for 30-45 minutes, then fluff with a fork. Prepare parmesan topping if desired. In a large skillet, sauté onion and celery in 1-2 T. of veg broth or water until softened, then stir in garlic. Chop mushroom stems and add to the onion mixture. Simmer until softened, then stir in rosemary, sage, thyme, salt, and pepper. Stir in cooked rice and remove from heat. Stir in chopped cranberries and vinegar, then stuff each mushroom with the mixture. Top with vegan parmesan. Bake stuffed mushrooms for an additional 20 minutes and serve.

SUGAR-FREE CRANBERRY SAUCE WITH SWEET CHERRIES ★

6 medjool dates
12 oz. cranberries
1 c. frozen dark sweet cherries
1 T. orange zest
1 cinnamon stick

¼ tsp. ground ginger
¼ tsp. nutmeg
¼ tsp. allspice
1 c. orange juice

Cover your dates with hot water and allow them to soak until softened, at least an hour or so. Rinse and drain your cranberries and then add them to a large soup pan. Add the dark cherries, orange zest, and spices. Finally, blend the dates with 1 cup of orange juice until smooth and pour into the pan. Adjust the heat to med-high until the cranberries begin to pop, then reduce the heat to a slow simmer for 10 minutes, stirring occasionally. Remove from heat and allow to cool. The sauce will thicken as it cools. Adjust seasoning to taste. If you like a sweeter sauce, you can add a few more cherries or blend in another date.

VEGAN DRESSING ★

1 c. onion
1 c. celery
½ c. green bell pepper
1 c. portobello mushrooms
½ tsp. onion powder
½ tsp. marjoram
½ tsp. oregano
½ tsp. thyme

¼ tsp. black pepper
2 T. rubbed sage
1 (12 oz.) pkg. dressing mix or 12 c. stale, day-old, bread cubes
3 c. low-sodium vegetable broth
¼ c. Italian parsley

Preheat oven to 350° F. Dice onion, celery, and pepper and add to a large pot. Slice mushroom and add to pot. Sauté veggies in a small amount of water/broth until softened. Add onion powder, marjoram, oregano, thyme, pepper, and sage and stir until fragrant - about 1-2 minutes. Remove from heat. Add a small amount of bread cubes/stuffing mix and broth at a time, mixing well. Alternate bread/broth until all of the cubes and broth have been incorporated and there are no dry pieces of bread anywhere. Use just enough broth to moisten. Stir in chopped parsley and line a 9" x 13" baking dish with parchment paper. Spoon dressing into the pan and smash down as necessary to get it all to fit. Cover with additional parchment paper if desired, and aluminum foil to retain the moisture. Bake covered for 30 minutes. Remove foil/parchment and bake uncovered for an additional 10 minutes.

VEGAN SOUP BEANS

16 oz. dried pinto beans
1 onion
3 cloves garlic, minced
4 c. water
4 c. low-sodium vegetable broth

1 tsp. liquid smoke
1 tsp. onion powder
½ tsp. cumin
¾ tsp. salt
¼ tsp. black pepper

Pick over beans removing any twigs, deformed beans, dirt, etc. Rinse well and then place in a large pot and add just enough water to cover. Let soak overnight. The next day, drain the beans, rinse well, and return them to the pot. Add diced onion, garlic, water, broth, and all the seasonings EXCEPT the salt and pepper. Bring to a boil, reduce heat to a simmer, and cover. Check beans every hour to ensure there is plenty of liquid. Beans should be tender in 3-4 hours. Season with salt and pepper.

Soups & Stews

Thank You!

Thank you for purchasing this cookbook!

Your support is what made this book possible, and as it is my very first *real* book, it really means the world to me!

And thank you for your patience since I completely self-published this book. I hope I didn't keep you waiting too long.

I sincerely hope you enjoy the recipes.

If you would like to follow me on any of my social channels or support groups, I have left all the links below.

Website: https://www.brandnewvegan.com
Facebook: https://facebook.com/brandnewvegan
FB Group: https://www.facebook.com/groups/bnvcommunity
Instagram: https://www.instagram.com/brandnewvegan
YouTube: https://www.youtube.com/brandnewvegan
Support Group: https://bnvcommunity.com
Substack: https://brandnewvegan.substack.com
Email: chuck@brandnewvegan.com
Address: Chuck Underwood: Brand New Vegan, PO Box 251, Cornelius, OR 97113

Medical Disclaimer

This book is intended to provide helpful general information on the vegan diet and lifestyle. It is not a substitute for the advice of the reader's own medical professionals based on the reader's own medical conditions and concerns.

The reader should consult trained medical professionals for personal medical, health, dietary, exercise, or other advice.

The author is not responsible for any injury, damage, or loss the reader may experience, directly or indirectly, as a result of following any recipes, directions or suggestions in this book.

SOUPS & STEWS

BEST DAMN VEGAN CHILI

1 lg. onion
1 red bell pepper
1 green bell pepper
3 cloves garlic, minced
½ c. bulgur wheat (opt.)
1 (15 oz.) can fire-roasted tomatoes
1 (8 oz.) can tomato sauce
2 c. low-sodium vegetable broth
¼ c. generic chili powder
2 tsp. ground cumin
1 tsp. paprika
1 tsp. oregano
½ tsp. garlic powder
½ tsp. onion powder
salt & pepper to taste
1 c. vegetarian refried beans
1 (15 oz.) can pinto beans
1 (15 oz.) can kidney beans
2 T. pickled jalapeños with juice (opt.)
1 T. masa harina (opt.)

Chop onion and peppers and put into a large soup pot or Dutch oven. Sauté in a little veggie broth until translucent and softened. Add minced garlic and sauté for an additional 30 seconds until fragrant. Add any kind of meat substitute (if using) or dry, uncooked bulgur and continue to stir for a few minutes until heated through. Add tomatoes, tomato sauce, and remaining broth. Add in spices and stir until mixed well. Add all the beans (draining and rinsing pinto beans only) and jalapeños and stir. Sprinkle up to 1-2 T. of the masa on top if you think it needs thickening. The masa adds a slight "corn tortilla" or "tamale" flavor to the chili. Give the chili one more good stir and bring it to a slow boil. Reduce heat, cover, and simmer for 15 to 30 minutes.

CABBAGE SOUP

1 lg. yellow onion
4 cloves garlic, minced
2 ribs celery
1 carrot
1 parsnip
1 (10 oz.) pkg. frozen green beans
2 (15 oz.) cans fire-roasted tomatoes
½ head green cabbage
4 c. low-sodium vegetable broth
2 c. water
½ bunch fresh Italian parsley
1 tsp. oregano
½ tsp. thyme
½ tsp. salt
¼ tsp. black pepper
1 T. balsamic vinegar

Soften diced onion and minced garlic in a large 6-qt. stock pot. Add diced celery, carrot, parsnip, green beans, and both cans of tomatoes. Simmer for 10 minutes while you chop the cabbage. Add chopped cabbage, veg broth, water, parsley, oregano, and thyme. Stir well and bring to a boil. Once the soup has come to a boil, reduce heat and cover. Simmer 20-25 minutes. Season with salt, pepper, and balsamic vinegar.

HEARTY MINESTRONE ⓖⓕ

- 1 med. onion
- 2 ribs celery
- 2 med. carrots
- 4 cloves garlic
- ¼ c. tomato paste
- 1 (28 oz.) can diced tomatoes
- 2 c. low-sodium vegetable broth
- 2 c. water
- 1 (15 oz.) can kidney beans
- 1 (15 oz.) can navy beans
- 1 c. green beans
- ½ c. gluten-free pasta
- ½ tsp. Italian seasoning
- ½ tsp. thyme
- ½ tsp. salt
- ¼ tsp. pepper
- 2 bay leaves
- 2 T. red wine vinegar

Dice the onion, celery, and carrots. Over medium-low heat, add enough veg broth to cover the pan bottom and sauté onion, celery, and carrots until softened. Add garlic and stir for 1 minute. Add tomato paste and stir for 1 minute. Add tomatoes, broth, and water and stir. Add rinsed and drained beans and pasta. Add seasonings and mix well. Cover and bring to a boil. Just as it comes to a boil, turn down the heat to low, cover, and simmer for 30 minutes. Stir in red wine vinegar right before serving.

Garlic is as good as having ten mothers.

- Old Saying

HEARTY VEGETABLE STEW

Roux

1 sm. onion
1 carrot
1 clove garlic, minced
1 rib celery
¼ c. low-sodium vegetable broth

Stew

1 lg. onion
16 oz. portobello mushrooms
1 tsp. rosemary
1 tsp. Italian seasoning
½ c. red wine
3 c. low-sodium vegetable broth
1 (15 oz.) can diced tomatoes
1 (8 oz.) can tomato sauce
2 med. carrots
2 ribs celery
2 Yukon gold potatoes
½ tsp. salt
¼ tsp. black pepper
1 T. balsamic vinegar
1 c. frozen peas
1 T. cornstarch

Finely mince the carrot, celery, and small onion for the roux. Sauté this mixture in ¼ cup of veg broth until the veggies are nice and soft. Add the large chopped onion and continue cooking until softened. It's ok if the liquid gets a little low - the brown bits add to the flavor. Dice and add the mushrooms and cook on medium-high until they lose their liquid. Season with rosemary and Italian seasoning. Add the wine and deglaze any brown spots in your pan. After a few minutes, add the rest of the broth, the tomatoes, and the tomato sauce. Chop the carrots, celery, and potatoes, add to the pot, and turn the heat up to boil. Add the rest of the seasonings - but not the cornstarch. Once mixture is boiling, turn down the heat to low and add the peas. Mix the cornstarch with a tablespoon of cold water and stir this in to thicken. Simmer to desired consistency.

MISO SOUP

4" square kombu seaweed
4 c. water
¼ c. dried shiitake mushroom powder
4 T. red miso
8 oz. extra-firm tofu
1 T. low-sodium soy sauce
½ c. sliced green onions
1-2 T. wakame or dulse seaweed
½ c. shredded kale

Add the 4" piece of kombu to 4 cups of water - bring to almost boiling and then turn down heat. Whisk in mushroom powder and simmer/stir until smooth. Strain (or just remove kombu). Whisk in the miso and make sure to break up any clumps. Cut tofu into small cubes, and add soy sauce, tofu, and green onions to the pot. Gently stir to mix. Add wakame, or dulse, or kale and simmer until just wilted.

SPINACH SOUP

- 1 onion
- 2 ribs celery
- 2 russet potatoes
- 1 (7 oz.) can roasted green chiles
- 2 cloves garlic, minced
- ½ tsp. salt
- ½ tsp. garlic powder
- ½ tsp. thyme
- ½ tsp. oregano
- 2 bay leaves
- ½ c. riced cauliflower
- 4 c. low-sodium vegetable broth
- 1 (16 oz.) bag baby spinach
- ¼ tsp. nutmeg
- pickled jalapeños for garnish (opt.)

Add diced onion, celery, potato, green chiles, and a splash of veg broth to a large soup pot. Cook on medium until veggies start to soften - 5 minutes. Add garlic, salt, garlic powder, thyme, and oregano and stir. Cook for 1 minute. Add bay leaves, cauliflower, and veg broth, stir, and cover. Cook for 10 minutes. Add spinach. Stir, cover, and cook for 6 minutes - stirring occasionally. Stir and taste for seasoning. Add nutmeg. Working in batches, transfer to a blender and blend until smooth and creamy. Serving suggestions: Garnish with pickled jalapeños. Serve over rice, with crusty bread.

THREE SISTERS STEW

- 1 (15 oz.) can kidney beans
- 1 (15 oz.) can corn
- 1 red onion
- 2 cloves garlic, minced
- 1 tsp. oregano
- 1 tsp. cumin
- ½ tsp. garlic powder
- ½ tsp. onion powder
- 1 (7 oz.) can diced green chiles
- 1 c. diced Yukon gold potatoes
- 2 c. diced butternut squash
- 2 c. low-sodium vegetable broth
- 1 (15 oz.) can diced-tomatoes
- 2 c. water
- small handful cilantro or parsley

Drain and rinse the beans and corn. Dice the onion and add it to a large soup pot or Dutch oven. Simmer onion over med-low heat until softened. Add minced garlic and stir until fragrant - about 30 sec., then add the spices and mix well. Add the diced chiles and stir to combine. Add diced potatoes and stir to combine - add water or broth if needed. Peel squash and dice into the same sized cubes you used for the potatoes. Stir squash into the stew and add the broth. Add the drained corn and beans and stir. Add the tomatoes and stir. Add 2 cups of water and mix well. Bring to a low boil, then cover and reduce heat to simmer. Simmer for 30-45 minutes or until vegetables are tender. Add a small handful of parsley or cilantro for garnish and salt & pepper to taste.

VEGAN BROCCOLI CHEDDAR SOUP

1 med. head cauliflower
1 c. carrot
1 med. Yukon gold potato
3 ribs celery
¼ onion
4 c. low-sodium vegetable broth
½ c. unsweetened almond milk

½ c. nutritional yeast
2 T. lemon juice
1½ T. apple cider vinegar
1 tsp. garlic powder
¾ tsp. salt
¼ tsp. black pepper
10 oz. frozen broccoli

Chop all vegetables (except broccoli) and add to soup pot. Add the vegetable broth and bring to a boil. Cook until vegetables are soft and then carefully blend soup using a blender or immersion blender. Stir in milk and all seasonings and mix well. Adjust any seasonings as necessary and then add frozen broccoli. Simmer on low heat for 5-10 minutes until broccoli is heated through. Serve with your favorite bread or salad.

VEGAN BUTTERNUT SOUP

1 lg. onion
5 cloves garlic
2 carrots
1 (3.5 lb.) butternut squash
4 c. low-sodium vegetable broth
2 c. water
1 T. maple syrup
½ tsp. salt

½ tsp. Italian seasoning
½ tsp. rubbed sage
2 T. apple cider vinegar
garnish with favorite toppings, including roasted pumpkin seeds, cashew cream, parsley, or chives

Preheat oven to 400° F. Peel onion and cut into quarters. Peel garlic cloves. Clean carrots and cut into 3-4 pieces and arrange all veggies on a parchment lined baking sheet. Carefully cut squash lengthwise into 2 equal pieces, and remove seeds & pulp. Arrange squash, cut-side UP, next to veggies, sprinkle with a little salt, and roast for 1 hour. Allow squash to cool enough to safely handle. Scoop out the cooked squash (discarding the skin) into a large soup pan or Dutch oven and add the other roasted veggies. Add veg broth, water, maple syrup, salt, Italian seasoning, and sage and bring to a boil. Reduce heat to a steady simmer and cook for 30-45 minutes. Blend in batches, or using an immersion blender, until smooth. Add apple cider vinegar and salt to taste. Serve with your favorite garnish like roasted pumpkin seeds, cashew cream, parsley, chives, etc.

VEGAN IRISH STEW

1 lg. yellow onion
2 ribs celery
1 carrot
1 parsnip
3 cloves garlic, minced
16 oz. portobello mushrooms
¼ c. tomato paste
1 (12 oz.) bottle stout beer
3 c. low-sodium vegetable broth
12 oz. baby potatoes

2 bay leaves
1 T. vegan Worcestershire sauce
1 tsp. dried thyme
½ tsp. dried rosemary
½ tsp. salt
¼ tsp. black pepper
2 T. cornstarch
1 T. water
garnish with fresh parsley

Dice onion and add to a stew pot or Dutch oven. Soften onion in a few tablespoons of veg broth. Add chopped celery, carrot, and parsnip - simmer for 5 minutes. Add minced garlic and stir. Clean mushrooms and cut them in half. Add mushrooms to the pot and simmer until slightly reduced in size. Stir in tomato paste and add beer. Stir well and simmer for 1-2 minutes. Add broth and baby potatoes that have been cut in half. Add all seasonings and bring to a slow boil. Reduce heat and cover. Simmer for 20-30 minutes or until potatoes are cooked through. Mix cornstarch and water and stir into stew to thicken. Garnish with fresh parsley if desired. Serve with your favorite crusty bread.

VEGAN WHITE BEAN SOUP

1 yellow onion
2 cloves garlic, minced
2 ribs celery
2 carrots
2 tsp. basil
1 ½ tsp. rubbed sage
salt & pepper to taste

3 ½ c. low-sodium vegetable broth
½ c. unsweetened almond milk
3 (15 oz.) cans white beans
1 (15 oz.) can diced tomatoes
3 handfuls baby spinach

Chop the onion, garlic, celery, and carrots and add to a large soup pan. Sauté in a little veg broth or water until the onion is softened. Season with basil, sage, salt, and pepper. Add the veg broth and almond milk and stir to combine. Rinse and drain the beans and add to the soup. Cover and simmer on med-low for 20 minutes. Rinse and drain the tomatoes and fold them into soup. Roughly chop 3 handfuls of baby spinach and add to soup. Remove from heat and allow spinach to wilt. Purée 2 cups of soup in a blender and add back in the soup pan for a thicker soup.

INDEX OF RECIPES

APPETIZERS & SNACKS

BBQ CAULIFLOWER WINGS	1
CRISPY BAKED ONION RINGS	1
GRILLED VEGETABLE KABOBS ⊛	2
JALAPEÑO POPPERS 🌶	3
LITTLE SMOKIES COCKTAIL CARROTS ⊛	4
SIMPLE POLENTA BRUSCHETTA ⊛	4
VEGAN NACHOS SUPREME ⊛	5

BREADS

HERB CRUSTED PIZZA DOUGH	7
HOMEMADE CORN TORTILLAS ⊛	7
HOMEMADE POTATO ROLLS	8
OATMEAL APPLESAUCE MUFFINS	8
RUSTIC NO-KNEAD BREAD	9
SIMPLE VEGAN CORNBREAD	9
VEGAN FLUFFY BUTTERMILK BISCUITS	9

DIPS & SPREADS

BASIC OIL-FREE HUMMUS ⊛	11
BRAND NEW VEGAN GUACAMOLE ⊛	11
CORN BUTTER ⊛	11
MEXICAN STREET CORN DIP ⊛	12
OIL-FREE COWBOY CAVIAR ⊛	13
PIZZA HUMMUS ⊛	13

MAIN DISH - ASIAN

ASIAN STIR FRY SAUCE	15
CREAMY GARLIC MISO NOODLES	15
EASY VEGAN PAD THAI	16
EASY VEGAN PEANUT NOODLES	16
HOT AND SOUR SOUP	17
KOREAN BRUSSELS SPROUTS	17
KOREAN MAC N CHEESE 🌶	18
MONGOLIAN SOY CURLS	19
VEGAN ORANGE CHICK'N	20
VEGAN PEPPER STEAK ⊛	21

MAIN DISH - CLASSICS

AMAZING CAULIFLOWER TACO CRUMBLES	23
CREAMY MUSHROOM STROGANOFF	23
CREAMY VEGAN MAC & CHEESE	24
SAVORY MUSHROOM POT PIE	24
SHEPHERDESS PIE	25
TACO PIE	25
VEGAN CHICK'N & DUMPLINGS	26
VEGAN CHICK'N POT PIE	27
VEGAN HAMBURGER HELPER	27
VEGAN LASAGNA WITH TOFU SPINACH RICOTTA	28
VEGAN MEATLOAF ★	29

MAIN DISH - MEXICAN

BLACK BEAN TOSTADAS WITH GREEN CHILE SOUR CREAM 🌶	31
CHEESY HASH BROWN ENCHILADAS	32
EASY NEW MEXICAN RED CHILE SAUCE (ENCHILADA SAUCE) 🌶	32
GALLO PINTO (VEGAN RICE & BEANS)	33
HATCH GREEN CHILE SAUCE 🌶	33
MEXICAN 7 LAYER DIP ⊛	34
MEXICAN PASTA SALAD ⊛	34
POSOLE 🌶	35
SOPA DE FIDEO	35

MAIN DISH - POTATOES

BREAKFAST POTATOES	37
COTTAGE FRIES	37
CRISPY OVEN-BAKED FAT-FREE FRENCH FRIES	38
EASY DEVILED POTATOES ⊛	38
FAT-FREE POTATO CHIPS ⊛	38
FUNERAL POTATOES	39
HASH BROWN PIZZA CUPS	40
POTATO ENCHILADAS	40
SMASHED POTATOES WITH GARLIC AIOLI ⊛	41
SPICY ADOBO POTATOES 🌶	41

VEGAN POTATO SOUP WITH GREEN CHILES ⊛	42
VEGAN SWEET POTATO CASSEROLE ★	43
VEGAN SWEET POTATO CHILI	44

MAIN DISH - TOFU

BBQ TOFU BURNT ENDS	45
CHICK'N FRIED TOFU	46
EASIEST VEGAN STIR FRY EVER	47
GARLIC PANKO TOFU	48
MY GRANDSON'S FAVORITE TOFU	48
SPICY AIR-FRIED GARLIC TOFU 🌶	49
SPICY GENERAL TSO TOFU ⊛	50
TOFU TACOS	51
VEGAN MAPO TOFU	51

MULTICOOKER RECIPES

15 BEAN SOUP	53
BLACK BEAN SOUP	53
HOPPIN' JOHN	54
IRISH COLCANNON	54
PERFECT VEGGIE RICE	55
SMOKY COWBOY BEANS	55
SOUTHWESTERN SQUASH & CORN SOUP	56
SPANISH RICE	56
VEGAN REFRIED BEANS	57

SALADS & DRESSINGS

CREAMY VEGAN COLESLAW	59
FAT-FREE VEGAN POTATO SALAD ⊛	59
OIL-FREE PASTA SALAD	60
OIL-FREE VEGAN CAESAR DRESSING	60
VEGAN GREEK SALAD WITH TOFU FETA	61
VEGAN RANCH DRESSING	61
VEGAN THOUSAND ISLAND DRESSING	62

SANDWICHES & WRAPS

CHICKPEA SALAD (VEGAN TUNA SALAD)	63
ITALIAN SAUSAGE AND PEPPERS	64
MUSHROOM REUBEN	65
PORTOBELLO FRENCH DIP	66
SMOKY MAPLE TOFU BACON	66
SMOKY VEGAN CARROT DOGS ★	67
SPICY SOUTHWESTERN BLACK BEAN BURGER 🌶	67
VEGAN BANH MI SANDWICH 🌶	68
VEGAN BEER BRATS	69
VEGAN GYROS WITH TZATZIKI SAUCE	70

SAUCES & GRAVY

AMAZING VEGAN CHEESE SAUCE	71
BEST EVER FAT-FREE VEGAN GRAVY	71
BOLOGNESE SAUCE	72
OIL-FREE MARINARA SAUCE ⊛	73
ULTIMATE FAT-FREE PIZZA SAUCE	73
VEGAN COUNTRY SAUSAGE GRAVY	74
VEGAN GARLIC AIOLI SAUCE	74
VEGAN MUSHROOM GRAVY	75
VEGAN PARMESAN	75

SIDE DISHES

BEST DANG BBQ BAKED BEANS	77
SAVORY SUCCOTASH ⊛	77
SOUTHERN VEGAN GREEN BEANS	78
STUFFED MUSHROOMS ★	79
SUGAR-FREE CRANBERRY SAUCE WITH SWEET CHERRIES ★	79
VEGAN DRESSING ★	80
VEGAN SOUP BEANS	80

SOUPS & STEWS

BEST DAMN VEGAN CHILI	81
CABBAGE SOUP	81
HEARTY MINESTRONE ⊛	82
HEARTY VEGETABLE STEW	83
MISO SOUP	83
SPINACH SOUP	84
THREE SISTERS STEW ⊛	84
VEGAN BROCCOLI CHEDDAR SOUP	85
VEGAN BUTTERNUT SOUP ⊛	85
VEGAN IRISH STEW	86
VEGAN WHITE BEAN SOUP	86